Kudos for Jennifer Buchanan and TUNE IN

I've seen the beauty that can arise in the hearts of those that can not be reached by other types of therapy and yet they respond to the magic of music. Jennifer introduced me to the miracles that music therapy can perform. She has through her work touched many people in ways that could only be accomplished with both her special gift and her music - one of the most heart warming experiences of my life.

Don Felder,
Lead Guitarist of the Eagles

Jennifer is a great storyteller who effectively captures moments, making them fresh to the imagination.

The Rebecca Review

Jennifer brings an amazing perspective to how music can enrich every one of us. If you are trying to prevent disease or cope with disease, Jennifer's material will help you understand how music can truly bring happiness to your life.

Diamond Fernandes, Founder and Director,
Heart Fit Clinic

I salute you Jennifer in being a Music Therapist and working so tirelessly to help others in your community. Music is the universal language—and music therapy is so important as it is proven to have a significant impact on people's lives.

Melanie Berry, President and CEO,
Juno Awards and MusiCounts

The healing powers of music are both well-documented and practiced to tangible results throughout our world. Canada is so fortunate to have such a practitioner in Jennifer Buchanan. Professional, experienced, talented, and passionate, Jennifer is committed to ensuring that the healing powers of music thrive and are made accessible in new and innovative ways.

Andrew Moskar, President and CEO,
National Music Centre

D1715581

tune in

A Music Therapy Approach to Life

Use music intentionally to curb stress, boost morale, and restore health.

SECOND EDITION | REVISED AND EXPANDED

JENNIFER BUCHANAN

ISBN: 978-1-936449-69-9
Library of Congress Control Number: 2012940500

Limits of Liability and Disclaimer of Warranty
The author and publisher shall not be liable for your misuse of this material. This book is strictly for informational and educational purposes.

Warning—Disclaimer
The purpose of this book is to educate and entertain. The author and/or publisher do not guarantee that anyone following these techniques, suggestions, tips, ideas, or strategies will engender success. The author and/or publisher shall have neither liability nor responsibility to anyone with respect to any loss or damage caused, or alleged to be caused, directly or indirectly by the information contained in this book.

Except for family names and personal friends, names in the stories have been changed. Some stories are a composite of stories that the author has experienced in her music therapy career.

Cover and Interior Design: Andrea Lifton - www.CreativeLift.ca
Author Photo: Britta Kokemor Quinlan

((TUNE IN))
PRESS

to Granny and Grandad

"My idea is that there is music in the air, music all around us, the world is full of it, and you simply take as much as you require."
- Sir Edward Elgar

Foreword

Instinctively, we all know that music is powerful, that it has something magical about it. Put on the right song and you smile or cry, tap your feet, or just sigh a contented "ah."

Music connects to something deep within us, something that has to do with our ability as human beings to create anything we desire. I'm not just talking about art, music, or writing. Creating encompasses all of life—creating a cake or a clean space in your house, or even just creating an emotion, good or bad. Music gives us a direct conduit into that force and helps it blossom in a way that's almost unexplainable.

I had heard of the term "music therapy," a while ago, but never really paid attention—even dismissed it because of the word "therapy" to be honest (how could something so wonderful as music be reduced to therapy—like psychoanalysis or something). Then I met Jennifer Buchanan. She's a Music Therapist by training, but there was something about Jennifer that made me immediately sit up and pay attention. She talked about music in a way that I had not heard before. It was getting close to that "unexplainable" thing that I had always known existed with music but could never really put my finger on.

Jennifer definitely had a book inside her, itching to get out. I had never read a "music therapy" book, but I could tell that she was trying to get at something that hadn't been fully expressed before in writing. I told her that the science of music wasn't what made the topic interesting to me. As she started telling me her stories, I knew that in those stories lay the answer: it was what music could do to a being, a person who was in need of cheering up, of de-stressing, of even finding a way to connect back to the world.

Four years have passed since I first met Jennifer and two years since we published the first edition of this book. After I had read some preliminary drafts, I gave her some suggestions on how to enhance the message. After reading her book I thought a lot about music and how it was lacking more than a little in my life. I love music—I grew up playing the piano. I couldpick up just about any instrument, except the guitar for some reason, and learn how to play it pretty quickly. But I stopped listening to music consistently more than a few years ago. I didn't play the radio in the car because

I liked the silence. As a writer, sometimes I am consumed with my thoughts. I talk about "hearing" a book in my head before I write it, so I guess you could say I'm constantly writing, no matter what else I'm doing.

But since reading the first drafts of TUNE IN, I had been slightly bothered by the idea that I didn't listen to music that much anymore, and I certainly didn't listen to anything that uplifted me. I have a grade-school aged daughter so we listen to a lot of pop music but not much else.

Then one Sunday morning, I came home from the grocery store. My beloved father had died about three weeks earlier; I was buried in work, and I wasn't particularly happy—just doing my chores, making sure my family was taken care of.

As I walked in the door, I heard the wonderful sound of James Taylor singing "Sweet Baby James." We have a little boom box in our kitchen, nothing fancy, and my husband had put on a James Taylor Greatest Hits CD he had found in a thrift store the day before. As I listened to the strains of that song, I almost cried. It was the most beautiful thing I had heard in a long time. For whatever reason, on that morning that was "my" music, and the message of Jennifer's book hit me in the gut. When I needed something soothing, there it was: James Taylor singing to my soul. I felt immediately more relaxed. I put down the sack of groceries I was carrying and made my husband dance with me in the middle of the kitchen. I felt more connected to life than I had in a while. It is a memory I will cherish.

TUNE IN is all about using music intentionally. You'll hear a lot more about that in the following pages, but I'm sure you know instinctually what it means already. It's finding the right music for whatever situation: for when you're feeling blue and want to feel blue or when you need cheering up, for helping you through a tough spot in life or finding a way to make a difficult decision. It's dancing your way out of your kitchen—or wherever—because you have a reason to celebrate or "just because."

The greatest thing about music is that it is intensely personal. There is no "right" or "wrong" answers in finding the right music to help you in whatever situation you find yourself in. I hope, however, that by reading

TUNE IN, you'll have a better handle on understanding what music can do for you and how to use it more effectively and purposefully in your life.

I don't know if anyone can ever explain fully why music is so powerful. I do know that when you use music intentionally, you are tapping into a power source within you that knows no bounds.

Happy reading—and happy listening!

Dr. Patricia Ross, Publisher
Hugo House Publishers, Ltd,
Denver, 2015

Table of Contents

First Note

My granny was perfect. Truly. Everything about her said, "I know what I'm doing and you are in the best care." Her house was immaculate and her garden always looked like something out of a magazine. She seemed to have a secret way of knowing exactly where to plant each variety of plant or flower so that there was an explosion of colour throughout the year from the early spring through late summer. The only thing better than the visual aesthetic of her house was the smell of the baking that wafted continually from the kitchen. She was wonderfully generous with her love, and it showed in all that she did.

Grandad, her husband, was the complete opposite. While Granny made sure we were all well looked after, Grandad tucked himself away in the basement where he spent endless hours in his workshop far from the visiting grandchildren. When I did see Grandad, he always seemed grumpy. It would be many years before I would learn that his stern look was sparked by his resolve to be a successful provider, giving my dad and his brother what his parents were unable to give to him.

I don't remember Granny and Grandad laughing or talking together much but I do remember them hosting many family gatherings including BBQ's, Christmas parties, and Sunday dinners. I loved it when all my cousins would get together to play while distant, lively, quirky aunts and uncles would laugh and debate politics. At dinner time we would all head to the buffet line for roast beef, ham, and heaping bowls of white potatoes enthusiastically doused in gravy. Through it all the stereo would play an endless array of classics until someone started to play the piano. On leaving Granny's house you could count on three things: you were full, you had a great time, and you felt loved. I didn't know it then but this "era of perfection" was about to change.

I was twelve and my parents were on the brink of signing their divorce papers when Mom received a phone call informing us that Grandad had been rushed to the hospital. At the age of sixty-two, Grandad suffered a stroke that left him partially paralyzed and unable to speak. His status was touch and go for a week and although he recovered some, he would neve return home. In those days, there was no place for him to go except the local extended-care hospital.

Over a short period of time Granny and Grandad's beautiful home and garden went up for sale and Granny moved into a small apartment. She acquired her driver's licence (something she never felt she needed before) in order to visit Grandad at 7:00 a.m. each day. At night she cooked, and in the morning she transferred his favourite dishes and smells of home to the hospital. She brought fresh flowers for the dresser and his favourite comforter for the bed—all in an attempt to find a normalcy amongst the feeding tubes and daily therapies. Through it all, I never saw Granny shed a tear.

Mom had never known her own parents, and so she knew the importance of family ties for her children. Although there was stress around the impending divorce, we continued to visit Granny and Grandad at our allotted time slot: every Friday evening. However, after a couple of years of regular Friday visits, I discovered I had a different agenda, one that was full of friends, movies and social night outs. The last place I wanted to go was some hospital full of old people.

"Mom, I really don't want to go," I brooded.

"It is your Granny and Grandad and it means so much to them that we visit," said Mom.

"I don't think Grandad cares. The place smells bad, and I hate it when people try to touch me."

"Well this is what our family does, so get cleaned up and we'll grab a bite to eat on our way out." And that was that.

My mom, sister, and I would embark on the three-quarter hour trip. Once there, we would walk through the sliding doors and even if I had been blindfolded I would have known where we were. The smell of the place was a mix of fruit puree, musty clothes, and urine. The care facility was also quite noisy with voices reverberating off the cinder block walls and some seniors crying or yelling while others walked aimlessly throughout the halls.

As we walked into Grandad's room, I would mumble a greeting to Granny and Grandad and then immediately zero in on the only interesting thing to me—the little black and white television set on top of the corner table. Mom sat near Grandad's bed and visited with Granny and Grandad. My sister and I on the other hand rarely interacted with the adults as we were too busy adjusting the rabbit ears of the television set desperate to tune into whatever we could find. Granny looked over at us from the corner of her eye. She wanted us to tune into something else—she wanted us to tune into Grandad.

One Friday, Granny walked over to me, gave me a hug, and handed me a piece of music, "Jenny, I brought this sheet music from home. It is your Grandad's favourite song. Would you please learn it and sing it to him next week?"

Her request took me off guard. It seemed like such an odd request. With some reluctance I said, "Sure." Little did I know that Granny was using a technique known to lure in the most distant teenager. She asked me to share something I felt accomplished at. Music was something that fired up my intrinsic reward centres and motivated me to engage with others—but of course I didn't know it at the time.

I arrived the following Friday with my guitar in hand. Granny pulled up a chair beside the bed where Grandad was resting and leaned down into his ear and said, "I've asked Jenny to sing a song I think you'll like."

Grandad looked puzzled when he turned towards me, and I wondered if he even knew who I was. I sat down beside him careful not to hit the side of his bed with the neck of the guitar.

Granny put her hand on my shoulder and said, "Go ahead dear." I felt nervous and looked down on my lap at the words to the song. It took me a moment and then I began to sing a song written so many years before I was born:

> There'll be blue birds over The White Cliffs of Dover
> Tomorrow just you wait and see
> There'll be love and laughter
> And peace ever after
> Tomorrow when the world is free.

The first thing I noticed was a change in the sounds around me. The typical commotion and loud conversations in the hallways stopped. Although my back was to the door, I could tell that some people were beginning to look in. One of the wandering patients came right into Grandad's room, stood beside me, and Granny gave him the chair available. It surprised me when this new guest started to sing the words that were still new to me. Even the woman who regularly yelled in the hallways stood behind me and began to sing. I had no idea so many people knew this song. Granny smiled and nodded for me to keep going:

> *The shepherd will tend his sheep*
> *The valley will bloom again*
> *And Jimmy will go to sleep*
> *In his own little room again.*
> *There'll be blue birds over*
> *The white cliffs of Dover*
> *Tomorrow, just you wait and see.[1]*

I finished the song and looked up from the words into Grandad's eyes. He was crying. He reached out for my hand and when I put my hand in his he squeezed it. It was the first time I felt any connection to Grandad. I looked around the room and knew something bigger was happening, something far more important than me being worried about whether or not I got to watch T.V.

Granny rested her hand on my shoulder and announced proudly to the room, "Jenny will be here to sing every Friday night." I couldn't help but smile. Although I couldn't describe what was going on, I knew the moment was important.

Fortunately for me, many more musical moments like this would be in my future—with all sorts of people, from many different backgrounds and at all stages of life. Little did I know that these hospital visits would eventually lead me toward a rewarding career as a Music Therapist where, after many years of school, I would learn how to use music to calm, connect, even change the behaviours of people including more broody teenagers and grumpy old men.

About TUNE IN

The fundamental purpose of this book is to help you use music intentionally and with purpose to feel better regardless of your position, affluence, ability, age or music background. This book is meant to show you how to use music to uplift your spirits and feel healthier.

There is no denying that stress is hurting us and in many cases killing us: 44 percent of North Americans feel more stressed than they did even five years ago with one in five classifying themselves under extreme stress. There is also evidence to indicate that work stress causes 10 percent of all strokes[1] and that three out of four doctor's visits are for stress-related ailments.[2]

The fundamentals of what I'm teaching in this book is rooted in over twenty years of experience as a Music Therapist, including my experiences working directly with clients and also the collective experiences of my team of Accredited Music Therapists. I know what music can do to alleviate even the most stressful situations. Thus the mission for this book is to help everyone understand what music is capable of doing when we allow ourselves to tune into its potential. Music provides the power to ultimately transform your stress, improve your productivity, and restore you to health.

The arts keep edging their way into healthcare and education as we realize their value. Unfortunately during economic downturns, the arts are the first to be released at the precise time we need them most. Although some may dismiss the arts as an unjustified expense, research supports that the use of the arts in health care is actually cost-effective. For example, a study done at Tallahassee Memorial Healthcare showed how music therapy reduced stress in children undergoing CT scans. The cost savings when using music therapy showed a reduction of $567 per procedure. The researchers estimated that a potential savings of $2.25 billion per year could be saved if music therapy was used throughout the United States during such procedures.[3,4]

I have witnessed how music can stop babies from crying and make great men start. I have seen music open doors to communication for someone unable to speak, and silence someone who normally has words for everything. There are countless opportunities for music to make a difference.

It can and does save health care dollars, but its effects go far deeper than its monetary value. I have personally witnessed individuals who are unhappy or distraught experience a complete turnaround after being exposed to twenty minutes of intentiondally listening to or playing their own music. They feel brighter, they are able to laugh about themselves or with others; they even have been able to set a goal they previously felt they were not capable of pursuing. That, to me, is priceless.

TUNE IN is meant to be a source of inspiration and a guide for individuals who not only like music but are curious about using music to help them cope with the day-to-day issues in their life that may be causing them stress, unhappiness, even depression. It is also a book that aims to speak to the society at large, encouraging all of us to find new ways to connect and be healthy. Music is one of those ways.

To guide you beyond this introduction, this book is organized as follows:

Part 1 addresses the power of music that can be witnessed in people's lives. The short stories illustrate people using music under extreme circumstances with surprising results.

Part 2 demonstrates the value of music to help you achieve your goals.

Part 3 introduces you to how music is a trigger to both good and bad emotional states, and how to use this information to your advantage.

Part 4 is about how to find the right music that you will use intentionally for health and wellness.

Part 5 is a call to action highlighting strategies and exercises to maximize your music, helping to tie everything together in a way that is personal and unique to you.

TUNE IN is about people and the music-based practices that have worked for them. Through their stories, I hope you find inspiration. Although the majority of the stories took place in a controlled music therapy setting, the general public has much to gain from reading about the outcomes and changes that are possible. After you learn how music triggers feelings and shifts attitudes, the strategies at the end of book are meant to help you use music, from this point forward, with greater intention, for the goal is simple:

I want you to feel better, empowered, and uplifted through music.
There is no sacred order to this book. Your interests and needs will dictate
where to begin. I hope you enjoy it.

Jennifer Buchanan 2015

CHAPTER ONE

The Power of Music

"Music is the moonlight in the gloomy night of life."
- Jean Paul Richter

Music seems to be significant in many people's lives. Many simply enjoy listening. Others perform or create music, and thus music is a central part of their work life. Still others know that music creates an emotional response and use it to that effect liberally. Music can set the tone in any room—think about the soft music in a restaurant or upbeat sounds at a retail store and how that makes you feel. Athletes often listen to music before competing to improve their performance, and many of us use music in our never-ending quest for relaxation. And let's not forget those unforgettable soundtracks to our favorite films. All we need to hear is a few bars from our favourite movie and we can imagine scenes in the movie like we were there watching it.

This truly illustrates the real value of music: it is determined by what it does to the person experiencing it. Our connection to music is intensely personal. Over the past several years the role of music preferences has strongly been linked to three important psychological functions. When we respond positively to the music we are listening to we are more likely to improve our performance on certain tasks, our imagination is peaked, and our emotional state is altered.[1]

It really doesn't matter what kind of music you listen to to enhance those functions. There are many different styles, or genres, of music. From classical, jazz, blues, rock & roll, rhythm and blues, to rap, hip hop, country, bluegrass, folk, house, new age, world, metal—the list is ever-expanding. The long list of music choices coupled with many people carrying devices that can play music on a moment's notice makes music more accessible than ever.

The value people place on music varies from person to person. Some people have a casual relationship with music. They listen to various kinds of music they enjoy but don't try to interpret it much more than that. Some people integrate music into every aspect of their life and miss it when it does not exist. Then there are those who analyze what the author of a song is trying to say through their music while others critique singers and songwriters and confidently suggest what is or is not worth listening to.

No one can tell you what music to listen to, or play, to help you get to where you want to be. Music can allow people to feel freedom or connected to others. Music can help us feel balanced and confident or soothed and relaxed. Music, the right music for the right moment, can make us feel better. Music also has the most amazing ability to tune us in to our values and beliefs, some even very deep-seated—and can bring them front and centre.

In the introduction, I talk about how the foundation of this book is stories, for it is only through stories that I can even begin to suggest the power that music can have on an individual. The following stories are about how powerful music can be to a person. They are about people who experienced great difficulty in their lives, but through music, found a way to find peace with their situation while connecting with others or in my case, myself.

Mr. Nicholwitz: Feel a Good Song

When I was eight years old, I woke up just in time to see two burly men carrying an upright piano into our living room. The following Saturday morning Mr. Nicholwitz arrived at our front door to teach me my first piano lesson.

We could count on Mr. Nicholwitz to arrive each week, precisely five minutes before the lesson was scheduled, wearing his uniform—a pin-striped suit, dark-rimmed glasses and a fedora hat. He was robust in every way, with a belt you could barely see tucked under his belly. As he walked up our driveway he would appear distracted as he stopped to glance at something on the lawn or to look up into the sky. But he never failed to carry a large folder with pages protruding haphazardly under his arm.

Just before Mr. Nicholwitz knocked on our door, my sister and I ran from the window we had been watching from, quickly carried the sturdy chair from the spare room, and placed it close to the piano. He entered the house, nodded a heartfelt good morning, placed his hat on the corner table, and very slowly lowered himself into the chair. I knew the piano lesson had started when Mr. Nicholwitz reached in his folder and with a look of surprise pulled out a seemingly random song. "Oh yes, this is a good one" he would say as he placed the sheet music on the piano stand.

Each piece may have been a surprise to him, but I can assure you, it was even more of a surprise to me. When playing an unfamiliar song, I was frequently stumped halfway through. Mr. Nicholwitz would smile, tap my shoulder, and comment, "Oh that was really good... we will come back to that song later... here try this one," and he would put that song away and pull out another seemingly random sheet from his folder.

Over time a pattern emerged and the seemingly random, unfamiliar pieces became dependable, familiar favourites. Every time Mr. Nicholwitz leaned back in his chair with his eyelids closed, I knew he was happily absorbed in the piece and that I was playing it well enough for him to feel it. His responses made me love the experience even more.

Not for one moment did I ever feel that I disappointed Mr. Nicholwitz when I couldn't play a portion of the song at speed or with the right flourish. Looking back, his teaching style was certainly unorthodox, but in spite of it, and perhaps because of it, music became my lifelong passion.

Mr. Nicholwitz was the beginning of me appreciating music in a different way. Sure I learned how to play the piano from him, but what he really taught me was how to see, hear, and feel music differently. With my first piano teacher, music became more than just entertainment or an outlet for pent-up energy. Every week he reminded me that music can go deep down inside someone and find a harmony in that person's soul—I saw that in Mr. Nicholwitz's face every time I played. For me, my piano lessons taught me over and over that music was important to me because it could create such a wonderful effect in someone else.

Brad: Open the Drapes to Feeling Better

When I entered his room, Brad was lying on the top of his bed covered in his pajama bottoms and well-worn Ramones t-shirt. The sun was shining brightly outside, but his thick orange curtains were pulled tightly across the window. You could not see anything through them. When I entered, it took a few seconds for my eyes to adjust to the dimness of the room. Two twin beds were pressed against parallel walls with a nightstand in between and a small clock radio on top. Brad's roommate was also in the room. His eyes were shut, and he was curled up towards the wall and well-hidden under his pillows and blankets. He did not move or speak for the duration of my visit.

Earlier that day I was asked by a member of the care staff to help Brad get motivated. "He needs something," she said with a flick of a hand in the direction of his room.

"He rarely goes out anymore. He just lies there."

Looking quickly at Brad's chart, I read that he was forty-six-years old and had spent almost half his life in healthcare facilities. Brad suffered from severe Post Traumatic Stress Disorder and chronic depression due to his service in the first Gulf War. When his doctor determined he could no longer look after himself, he was admitted into a long-term care facility for assessment. That was almost twenty years ago.

Brad was one of the youngest residents in this long-term care facility. His schedule was a lot like many of the other residents. Each day, he went to the breakfast room for 8:30 a.m. After breakfast, he went back to his room and listened to his radio until smoke break at 10:30 a.m. After his five- minute break he went back to his room, lay on his bed, and listened to the radio until noon when lunch would be served in the communal dining room. Twice a week he would watch a movie, take a walk, or go for a swim with care staff. He ate dinner precisely at 5:30 p.m., went out for another smoke break, watched television, and went to sleep. Every day was the same.

I met Brad on a Tuesday; he was somewhere between smoke break and lunch. I closed the door to the noisy hallway behind me. Even with the door closed, I could still hear cutlery clanking, wobbly food trays squeaking, and heavy footsteps stomping past the door. Brad didn't seem to pay much attention to the noise and when I asked him what he was doing he said, "Just listening to the radio."

The radio was almost inaudible. When I adjusted my hearing, I picked up on a few strains from John Cougar Mellencamp. After introducing myself, I was told it was okay if I stayed for "a little while," so I pulled up a chair.

Suddenly, I was startled by a large crash—a food cart collapsed in the hallway. Neither man flinched as if it was a regular happening. I took the opportunity to ask Brad what he thought about all the sounds around him including the sounds outside his door. He turned his head slightly toward the wall and shrugged his shoulders.

Our auditory environment is known to affect our health. There is no question that many, if not most, hospitals and care settings don't sound restful. Studies show that the occurrence of aggressive behaviour, disturbance of sleep, constant stress, fatigue and hypertension can be linked to excessive and frequent noise levels. Brad's lack of response to such a loud sound indicated to me that he was disengaged from his environment.

I described the crash I heard just minutes before and asked Brad to explain what it sounded like to him.

He looked thoughtfully at the wall and said very slowly, "well....I guess...unhappy...muddled up... and lonely." The last word was almost completely mute.

He then looked down at the floor and said a bit louder, "I noticed you brought a guitar in here."

"Would you like me to play a little?" I asked.

He nodded.

He leaned over, turned off the radio, and stared at my guitar. I put the strap over my head and set my hands in position to play the first chord of a James Taylor tune. Brad was silent throughout. When I finished, he lifted his head a little higher on the pillow so his shoulders were elevated. I could now see him more clearly. The lines on his face made him seem much older than his forty-six years. I took a couple of deep breaths and began to sing a Bob Dylan song.

By the end of that song, Brad had shifted his pillow over to the side and was partially sitting up in his bed. I took a couple more breaths and sang yet one more song, this time from the Rolling Stones first album release. Once more, there was silence at the end of the song.

Finally, Brad looked directly at me, smiled, and sat fully upright with his feet hanging on the side of the bed. "Wow, those are good ones," he said. He began to suggest more songs and smiled again when I said I knew the one he spoke of.

The more songs I played, the more Brad opened up. Eventually, every song he suggested was coupled with a personal story from his past. It wasn't long before I saw a clear picture of the man now sitting in front of me. Once upon a time, Brad was a fearless, strong, vibrant and independent man who desired something more from his life.

The hour went by very quickly. As Brad walked me to the front door, I noticed his eyes were glistening a little in the sunlight. He suggested a few songs for the following week and waved goodbye.

Many people have encountered feeling down or even feeling totally apathetic about life at some time or another in their lives. For Brad, chronic PTSD and depression robbed him of living independently, of having many friends his own age, and of feeling involved in what was happening in the real world.[2,3] When I first started working with him, his world was closed off by his dark orange drapes and cluttered soundscape. By helping him narrow his focus, live music raised the volume from what was being played on the radio and the crash of sounds around him. It allowed him to give more space to intentional listening, dialogue, and eventually silence. It didn't take long for Brad's energy to shift. Music being played and listened to intentionally helped him connect to a bigger world.

Michael's Mom: Out of the Chaos Comes the Calm

As the saying goes, "everything in moderation," and for Michael's mom this was a discovery about to be made. I noticed several things about Michael's environment that reminded me of many modern homes. There were "things" everywhere, including many toys that were colourful and loud. The whole house had been modified to become his play centre and learning centre, from the kitchen to the living room, bathroom, and basement. "Things" were everywhere. Anyone visiting for the first time may not even think that adults actually lived there.

Michael was four years old and had autism. His mom moved very quickly around the house. She darted in and out of different rooms to complete her household tasks all the while ensuring that Michael was safe in his home. I was contracted to work with Michael, but this story is more about his mom.

When I met Michael's mom for the first time she stood at the counter and kept looking over her shoulder at her son. She spoke in a fast, high-pitched voice and every sentence went up at the end, sounding more like a question than a comment. She spoke loudly when Michael started going somewhere he shouldn't, in an attempt to get his attention. He made no apparent acknowledgement of her. I found out a bit more about Michael, and then I asked her how she was doing. "I feel exhausted all the time. Sometimes I just want to sit in the middle of the floor, close my eyes, plug my ears and shut everything out." Her face was weary, and I couldn't help but think how familiar this sounded—many of my friends with young children were feeling the same.

I asked Michael's mom if she would prepare a small room in her house for our next session, removing as many play things as possible, leaving only big furniture. I explained that with the majority of the house so "full of life" I wanted to eliminate as many distractions as possible to see if we could connect with Michael together without the use of his "things".

The following week, I entered the room with just one large drum and placed it in the middle of the floor. I had two mallets with me. I kept one mallet beside me and with the other I began to drum a steady, consistent beat. Michael entered the room and immediately stood still. He moved forward looking at the drum and the mallet that struck it. Not once did he attempt to take the mallet from me. He then turned to face the wall, rocking slightly. His rocking was in perfect time to the beating of the drum. After a few minutes, he looked back toward the drum and, after staring at it for a bit, moved to another area of the room and began to rock again. He repeated this behavior several times until I changed the rhythm. Then he stopped, and I stopped. He looked at the drum again and I passed him the mallet. He began to beat the drum in the same steady pulse that I had started the session. I began to play with him.

Suddenly, Michael's mom entered the room and began to clap. She used her voice to encourage him to continue. The child's unsolicited interaction ceased and he began to rock to his own rhythm.

"It was so great to see Michael responding to something. Then he stopped as soon as I entered the room," she said. When she entered the room her face appeared desperate; she desperately wanted to see a son she could be engaged with. She wanted to see her son connect to his world in a way that she understood. She began to cry and said how overwhelmed she felt looking after a son who rarely, if ever, interacts with her. "By the time my husband comes home from work, I am too tired to give him any attention."

Terrance Hays and Victor Minichiello have written extensively about the contribution of music to self-identity and improve quality of life.[4] They identify six music dimensions: linking, life events, sharing and connecting, well-being, therapeutic benefits, escapism, and spirituality. Michael's mom hoped to feel more connected to her son through music. Her goal for Michael was to support the development of many basic social and personal skills required for his eventual independent living.

I quickly realized that Michael's mom needed music therapy as much as he did. I explained to her that music can help her feel more connected to her son, and it would also help her reconnect to herself. It would most certainly help her alleviate her own stress about her son.

The first step was to literally "tone down" Michael's living space. "Timbre is another word for tone." I explained, "and timbre and tempo can trigger the changes you want to make. All tones affect us differently." When we are stressed our voice sometimes gets louder, higher, and sharper in tone. With coaching Michael's mom's voice became slower, calmer, lower, and softer. We went on to discuss Michael's program and goals and then moved on to discuss the tone of her home.

We also discussed the energy shift when her other two children and husband came home in the early evenings. We talked about the goals she had for her entire family, not just Michael. We then strategized a plan to drastically change the auditory environment of her home. We put away all of the sound-based toys that would now be brought out for purposeful activities and then be put away again. We selected music that would be used throughout the week and put together a soothing playlist for Michael's mom to use after Michael's bedtime.

Two weeks later, she called, "I am feeling much more relaxed at home. It is not perfect, but there are moments when I feel less frantic and overwhelmed." She went on to say that, "The best part is, Michael is changing. He is not moving from room to room so frantically and we can actually be in the same room for a longer period of time."

I was hired to help Michael, but in the end, Michael's mom benefitted as much or more than her son. Prior to our work, she was affected by everything around her. Once she started using music with Michael and throughout her home, she felt some relief from being constantly stressed and overwhelmed.

When a person starts using music with purpose, it can move that person so easily in the direction they want to go.

Me: Move Through the Green Light

Several years before I met Brad, I spent fourteen months feeling low after the birth of my second child. I have discovered over the years that this is a very common trend in our society.

Over several months I felt less emotional and more flat—never getting too upset or too happy. Nothing bothered me, but nothing seemed to excite me either—a state of being that really isn't me. This dullness became reflected in my music. I stopped listening to music for pleasure. I didn't consciously decide to stop listening, I just didn't turn the music on.

When my beautiful daughter was born, I continued with life normally—or so I thought. I cared for my older son who was eighteen months, worked full time, arranged childcare, found time with my husband, and completed the laundry most weeks. I did not realize that many of our family meals were now coming out of a box, that I stopped making the bed regularly, that I no longer felt like visiting friends, and that I was feeling generally tired all the time while rarely sleeping through the night. I didn't even question why I was crying when I pulled my car to the side of the road to pull myself together. I just continued on with my day, forgetting I had taken the time to cry at all. The sleep deprivation was taking its toll.

One day, I pulled up to an intersection and waited a few minutes at the red light. I reached down and turned on my favourite radio station. As the upbeat music hit my eardrum, I immediately felt different. I realized in an instant that I had not turned on this radio station since the birth of my daughter fourteen long months before. After ignoring months of atypical behaviour, I suddenly realized that for me, not listening to music for a long period of time was a clear indicator of something gone wrong.[5]

In that moment, when I stopped at that red traffic light and decided to turn on my favourite radio station, I instantly felt a renewed energy that I had not had for quite some time. I remember smiling and feeling a lot lighter and brighter as soon as I started singing along to the music. The dull, disconnected feeling disappeared, and I never felt that way again.

There are many indicators of extra stressors in our lives that make it hard to cope. Some are more recognized than others. Over the years, I have worked with many individuals like Brad, and even myself, who, after something happened in their lives, drastically changed their music listening habits or stopped listening to music altogether. Although some new research indicates that otherwise healthy and happy people may not enjoy and therefore not listen to music, I question whether there is something else happening in their lives that prompts them to keep music away. It would seem to me that music's capacity to reflect and evoke emotions and memories, some deeply hidden, may have something to do with the choice to live without any music.[6]

Music becomes a soothing agent during critical times. It is also an indicator of where we are emotionally. In my case, not listening to music revealed issues needing attention.

Donna and David: Clarity During a Difficult Time

For Donna, her greatest stressor was rooted in family. Donna's father had Alzheimer's Disease.[7] I have heard many people describe Alzheimer's as "as good as death." There are not many circumstances more stressful than the loss of a loved one. She told me, with tears in her eyes, "Three years ago I grieved the loss of my father. Today I care for a body that looks like him."

Donna, the youngest of three children, grew up in a small rural town helping her parents with the family farm. Her parents were almost forty when she was born. Donna moved away to the big city as soon as the opportunity arose. She married and settled into the family life she had always dreamed of. Her siblings had done the same while their parents remained on the farm.

When Donna's children were entering high school, her mom passed away and her dad was diagnosed with dementia. The family learned this disease would eventually kill him but no-one knew how long it would take.

With the encouragement of her husband and two teenaged children, Donna invited her dad to live with them.

Over the next three years, her dad's symptoms became more serious. He would forget where he placed his clothes or become very angry at the people who were caring for him. Eventually, Donna didn't feel comfortable leaving him alone and her family did not have the means to hire someone to help out. She realized that keeping her father at home was putting a strain on the entire family both emotionally and financially. She realized that a long-term care setting was the best option. At times, her guilt would get the better of her and she would say, "How could I send my dad to a place like that?"

I met Donna through the local senior's centre. Each month, Donna took her dad to a senior's centre for a "therapeutic drum circle," a music program I had especially designed for individuals with dementia and their caregivers.[8] Rhythmic and other similarly practiced responses require little to no cognitive processing. They are influenced by the motor center of the brain that responds directly to auditory cues. In the case of Alzheimer's or dementia, a person's ability to engage in music, such as drumming and singing, remains intact late into the disease process because these activities do not require cognitive functioning for feelings of achievement.[9]

Keeping this in mind, I placed drums and small percussion instruments in the middle of the circle of chairs. By 10:00 a.m., ten couples had entered and sat next to each other. Half of each duo held a calm but almost distant stare while the other half stood close-by, helped put on name tags, and assisted their loved-one into their chair. A few minutes before the group was about to start, Donna entered the room with David, her dad.

Donna was one of the younger members in the group; she always seemed vibrant while mingling around the room, making others laugh and feel welcome. I had known Donna and David for almost two years when Donna arrived looking exceptionally tired. After she found two chairs side-by-side, I walked over to her, pointed to another empty chair, and said, "Donna, that chair over there is available. I put a large drum in front of it for you to play. I will sit next to David."

With a mix of relief and concern, she kissed her dad on the cheek and went across the circle to the chair behind the big drum. David's drumming was in perfect time. It didn't take long for his normal vacant stare to be replaced with a calm, pleasant expression after just a few beats. This was usual; however, Donna was another story entirely. Although Donna's tired face didn't change, her movements grew stronger with every beat.

As the session continued, Donna went through a most amazing visible transformation. First, Donna closed her eyes; she obviously didn't want to notice anyone else. Within a few minutes, you could hear her drum over all the others. After an hour, the drumming came to a stop. She leaned back in her chair but kept her eyes closed.

After a brief silence I strummed a few chords on my guitar leading into a familiar song. David sang every word, often looking me in the eyes with a warm smile of recognition. When the song ended, I turned to David and asked, "How did the music make you feel today?" Without looking at me, his lips opened and closed several times. I looked across the circle at Donna who was about to speak for her dad. I put up a gentle hand signifying that it was okay and that she didn't have to answer for him. I repeated the question. "How did the music make you feel today?" David looked at me, smiled, and said, "Music makes me happy."

You could hear an audible exhale from those in the room who were patiently waiting for his answer. David smiled again. Donna, visibly relieved, leaned back in her chair and rubbed her hands after the intense drumming.

Donna walked me out to my car after helping her dad get into her vehicle. She shook her head and sobbed, "I can't do it, I can't do it." We stopped and looked at each other. I knew her dad had changed considerably over the past two years and seemed more distant and foggy. He had greater difficulty moving around and needed help standing up.

Donna dropped her chin to her chest and, still crying, told me, "I have applied to have him moved to a facility. I cannot look after him any longer—it is not fair to Ken or our children. The entire time I was playing the drum, I realized I was so mad at him. Well, not mad at him but mad at the disease for taking him away. I have been feeling guilty about my choice to move him into a care facility." She took a deep breath, looked back up at me, and said, "Today, all my feelings of guilt surfaced, but I know it is something I must do. I will find a good place and will commit to regular visits. I just wanted you to know."

Making tough choices on our own is highly stressful. Even though

Donna had siblings and a husband, she knew that at the end of the day, the responsibility for her father rested on her shoulders. We talked more about David's transition and that it would not be easy. Encouragingly, I reminded her that it had been done successfully by other people in similar situations, many times before. Donna relaxed, and we agreed to set up weekly music therapy sessions with David in his new home. Although it was a small piece of the pie, it provided Donna with some comfort.

Although music would never fix this problem, it provided a moment of clarity for Donna. She was able to express intense anger, regret, and guilt through the drum, without hurting someone else. I think music also gave both Donna and her father great comfort as his health waned. He continued to show us that music made him happy and that helped Donna through that most difficult transition of saying her final goodbyes.

Ruth and Warren: Celebrate the One I Love

Ruth never yelled or had a moment where she demonstrated frustration at another person. She smiled most days and every movement she made carried a happy lilt. Ruth's brown hair was now speckled with grey, and she kept it cut quite short so she didn't have to fuss too much with it. Her wide set eyes and low muscle tone indicated that she had some extra DNA on her twenty-first chromosome, better known as Down Syndrome.[10]

As if it was possible, Warren had an even broader grin than Ruth. He loved wearing baggy, corduroy pants and plaid shirts tucked in. His hair was completely white and you could easily envision that in his youth, he was a happy little blond boy who occasionally got into a bit of trouble. Warren's genetic makeup was also unique. Missing some DNA on his seventh chromosome, Warren had William's Syndrome.[11]

Both were in their late forties and had married each other five years previously. What surprised me most about their relationship was how happy the two seemed. They were more like honeymooners than a couple who had been married for half a decade. Neither seemed to be affected by what the rest of world deemed their ability "challenges." During one of our early conversations, they jokingly told me, "We feel great. Together we have the perfect number of chromosomes," and then chuckled knowingly.

Over the course of a weekend conference, Warren and Ruth participated in all the music activities organized for the participants. Naturally they captured my attention but not for the reason you may think. You see, I noticed that Ruth would not only walk behind Warren but would also stand slightly behind him and watch him as he sang. It didn't seem like she felt inferior to Warren but that she truly admired him. As Warren sang, her eyes would soften and she would clap enthusiastically when he finished. At times, she would join him in a chorus. Occasionally, she would sit back and observe him with a twinkle in her eye. Likewise, Warren would glance at his wife and, with a soft smile, hold her hand while gently swaying to the music. It seemed that Warren was performing for Ruth. She was his sole audience and they both loved it that way.

I am sure you know people like Ruth. They may not sing in tune or dance to the right rhythms, however, their passion for music is released every time they hear "their band" or "their song" and in Ruth's case when she heard "her love," Warren, sing and perform. Through music, Ruth could express her feelings openly, and her pleasure was infectious. She helped others enjoy the moment they were in by feeling her enthusiasm for the music she was hearing her Warren perform.

Intentional Music

In the introduction, I talked about the idea of using music intentionally. To do something with intention means that you do it purposefully with a goal in mind. Using music intentionally means that you aren't just passively listening to music because you like it or because it makes you feel better. Rather, you are choosing to use music in a way to improve your well-being. You have made yourself aware of the various effects music has on you and then consciously use music to help you in whatever way you need help in that moment.

The people I introduced you to in this chapter use music intentionally in their lives. This has made music far more valuable to them than just background noise or entertainment. Brad's personal soundtrack brought his personality out not only to me, but to others as well. He later told me that after I left that first day, he turned up the radio, changed the station, and started conversing with his roommate. This was a roommate he rarely spoke to even though he rested in a parallel position only two metres away. Brad used music to help himself bridge the chasm he felt between himself and the world. Over time and after subsequent sessions, Brad became more active and volunteered in the facility's kitchen so he could speak to people more often and spend less time in his room. He encouraged the kitchen staff to play music as they worked.

Michael's mom re-engaged with her home, her son, and I think most importantly herself when she learned how to use music effectively. She was able to find a sense of calm in her music which helped her create the right tone for her home.

After I travelled through the green light with music again playing out of the stereo, I had a new pep in my step and felt more alive in fourteen seconds than I had in the previous fourteen months. It took that low moment in my life to truly understand that not listening to music tells me as much about how I am feeling as much as listening to it does.

Donna knew she was feeling guilty, tired, and frustrated with her circumstances. After expressing these feelings even more loudly on drum, she was able to reach a decision that, although still not something she felt good about, she at least had some peace about, knowing it was the best under the circumstances.

For Ruth and Warren, music meant many things, but watching them that day, I was reminded that music can be used to celebrate what is right in front of us—most especially those we care about the most.

I have spent two decades using music therapeutically with families of very young children, teens coping with difficult times, adults who can't find the right words to say, and seniors who feel like shut-ins, isolated and alone. Using music intentionally can open doors for all people, regardless of age or circumstance, and that can lead to desired change: improved communication, decreased stress, or an improvement in mood. That alone makes music valuable—priceless even.

There is also a material value to music, however, that cannot be ignored. Many studies suggest substantial healthcare dollars would be saved if music was used in the daily care of individuals.[12] In the first large-scale review of four hundred research papers in the neurochemistry of music, a team led by Prof. Daniel J. Levitin of McGill University's Psychology Dept.

has been able to show that playing and listening to music has clear benefits for all aspects of health—both mental and physical. In particular, music was found to improve the body's immune system—this fact alone could save billions—and greatly reduce levels of stress. Listening to music was also found to be more effective than prescription drugs in reducing anxiety prior to surgery. This alone has far-reaching, positive effects. Music, in this sense, is a very inexpensive drug with few adverse side effects.[13]

Music—when its capabilities are understood, when it's used with the proper intention—can achieve miraculous results, expressing our deepest core values and providing healing to our bodies and minds. Whether music signifies celebration, a time to reflect, or like Brad, a way to connect to yourself and to the world, it has the potential to be so much more than we've previously imagined. You can use music in little bits or in large quantities, but however you use it, research and my own and other Music Therapists' long-experience shows that music in your life can help you define specific goals, triggers, and eventually strategies that will improve your health and wellness.

When I began to conceptualize this book, I kept coming back to the question "how do you teach people the value of music when they are not musicians?" The answer is surprisingly simple. Each one of us is capable, thanks to technology and music's accessibility, of bringing music out of the background and putting it front and centre where it can do amazing things for our health and life as we grow and age. It doesn't matter if you are a performer or in the audience, or how passionate you are when you hear a song or sing it live, music can tap into each of us in a unique way, and that is where the benefits lie.

Music can speak for us when we can't find the actual words to convey what we're thinking or feeling. It can help us identify and come to know better those things we value most. Music is there, always, for us to use as a tool to help us cope with our own unique life experiences. It can have a direct influence when the music itself is affecting us and can also be a metaphor for something bigger.

Most of all, music creates a direct line to areas in our life that need attention and to our desired emotional state. Connecting to the music that is important to us is the first step to having it help change our emotional state.

I hope the stories in this chapter will motivate you to pay more attention to the music you're listening to so that you can start using music not as passive background "noise" but an active tool to help you deal with whatever challenges are in your life.

Understanding music's value is the first step to really tuning in to music. The next step to using music intentionally is to take a look at how music affects us emotionally so that you can use music more proactively to help you when you need an emotional boost or if you're experiencing emotionally difficult times.

Music can take you where you want to go, if you know how to let it.

Exercise: To Decrease Stress

1. Start with identifying the music that soothes you most. The tempo and genre will be unique to you so don't think "oh this is too fast" or "too slow." If the music makes you feel better, then that's the music you need. Once you have a selection of five to six songs that induce the feeling of calmness, you are ready to begin.

2. Find a comfortable and quiet place to sit or lay down, preferably near the sound source, or wear a comfortable pair of headphones. Test the volume to ensure it is strong enough to capture your attention and low enough you won't hurt your eardrums.

3. Before turning on the music take a few minutes to observe your breathing. Re-adjust your body until you feel you are in a comfortable position, keeping aware of your breath as it moves in and out. As thoughts arise let them drift past; never let them linger for long. Bring your focus back to your breath and turn on your pre-selected music.

4. Slowly shift your focus entirely onto the music. Follow the melody; pay attention to the pauses in the music; acknowledge the comfort this music brings to you. Continue for twenty minutes.

5. Keep in mind that when we are the most stressed we may be inclined to view music listening as a waste of time. However, it is when we are the most inclined to push music away that perhaps we need it most. When you have the right resources available— the music that soothes with listening equipment that will allow you to relax into it, you will find this brief exercise can boost your productivity and better your mood by reducing stress. It's been proven helpful for others. I hope you find it works for you, too.[14]

CHAPTER TWO

The Value of Music

"Music was my refuge. I could crawl into the space
between the notes and curl my back to loneliness."
Maya Angelou

There's a great song from the 1970's titled, "I Got the Music In Me."[1] The whole song is about this "thing" that music does to us—because "I got the music in me," the song suggests, then I "ain't got no trouble in my life."

Music when used with the right intention really can help us relax and make our lives easier. Right before I stopped at that red light and turned on my favourite radio station, something changed for me. It was one of those unique moments when change was natural and spontaneous.

This is not always the case. Many people, like Brad, need extra support. Brad had been in a hospital for many years and was often disengaged from the people and experiences around him. The music he listened to connected to something deep within him that brought him out of his low state. By sharing the music experience with another, that meant something to him, he felt more alive. With music he was better able to feel and connect to those around him.

Music helps us to feel connected to our feelings, our environment or the people around us—to feel connected to a bigger experience, a memory or a person we love.[2] As strongly as music can be used to help us remember, perhaps it is equally as good at helping us forget the other things going on in our life just for a while. It doesn't get rid of the cause of the stress, but it can create space around our spirit, for a few hours or even for a few minutes, and give us relief from our stresses. We can use that space to help us find a glimpse of where we want to go and maybe even give us the resolve to find a way to get there.

As a Music Therapist, I'm always on the lookout for how music can help others, but like someone who doesn't always take my own advice, I oftentimes overlook when I need a music pick me up. When I am reminded of it, however, the enormity of how simple a tool music can be to help handle whatever situation I'm in can be astounding.

One summer a few years ago, I was having to manage significant staff changes during two new program deployments and was having a particularly difficult work week. During this demanding time, I won tickets to a local concert. The headliner was a country artist who I knew very little about except for one popular song on the radio. As the date approached, I began to wonder if my workload would allow me to go at all. I began to list all the reasons why I shouldn't go:

- I had barely heard of the artist.
- His music wasn't completely appealing to me.
- I could complete another four hours of work if I didn't go.
- I could go to bed earlier the night of the concert and get up early in the morning to finish my work.

My friend called the morning of the event and sounded really excited to get together. She said she would pick me up at 7:00 p.m. and quickly ended the conversation before I had a chance to change my plans. My procrastination became a commitment.

We arrived early and headed to our fourth row "VIP" seats. Our greasy chicken fingers and fries were balanced carefully on our knees while we reviewed the week's events and the stresses we were feeling at work. Frankly, we were quite oblivious to what was happening around us.

When the lights dimmed, my friend and I looked up and realized the crowd, mostly women, were standing up waiting in anticipation for the concert to start. As we were the only ones sitting, we quickly licked our fingers, hid the garbage under our seats, and stood up.

The lights moved across the stage, the drums and bass guitar revved up, and the audience buzz began to swell. We felt the energy and excitement as the crowd waited in anticipation for the country star to appear.

The performer ran onto the stage singing the first few lines of a song; however, you could barely hear his voice over the screaming audience. And then an amazing thing happened. The incomprehensible screaming turned into one voice—a twenty-thousand voice back-up group, singing every word of the melody. They sang not only the first verse, but every "red-necked, light-your-house-on-fire, put-the-dog-in-the-front-seat, let's-go-cruise-the-town" lyric for the next seventy-five minutes. I was amidst pure fan commitment. If you can sing along to an entire album of the Beatles, Elton John, the Police, Led Zepplin, or any artist you care to name, then you know exactly what I mean. In no time at all we were dancing and singing along to the repetitive choruses.

As I became a part of that audience who in turn became totally transfixed and completely connected to the musical moment and the person who brought it to them, my stress started to melt away. By the end of the concert our thoughts about work had vanished. For the first time in many days, I felt lighter, more connected to myself, and more connected to my friend with whom I shared the experience. Because I let myself enjoy the entire music experience, I was much more ready to face the next work day with a new vigour I did not have before.

Humans make decisions based on emotion and then construct the logic behind these decisions. A few years ago, neuroscientist Antonio Damasio made a groundbreaking discovery.[3] He studied people who had sustained damage to the part of the brain where emotions were generated. He found that they were no longer able to feel and express emotions. In addition they couldn't make decisions. They could describe what they should be doing in logical terms, yet they found it very difficult to make even simple decisions, such as what to eat. The field of neuroscience concluded that decision-making is not logical, it's emotional. Therefore, if you want to change someone's mind you first need to change their mood. The quickest way I know to change a person's mood is to add music to the relationship.

Sixties rock superstar Jimi Hendrix said: 'You can hypnotize people with music, and when you get them at their weakest point, you can preach into their subconscious whatever you want to say'.[4] After my grandfather suffered a stroke, he lost his ability to speak but not his ability to be miserable. After singing to my grandfather for the first time, he expressed softness towards me—something he had never shown me before.

Time after time I have witnessed people saturated in a moment of music that changes them—from crusty to relaxed, from lonely to secure, from uncomfortable to soothed. But how aware are you of how music affects your mood? Have you ever really thought about why you turn on the radio or listen to a particular CD? For many of us, putting on music is a reflex. We know we like music, but when we're doing something absent-mindedly, we don't really take time to analyze why we like a particular song or piece of music. We may turn the station or skip a track on the album because we don't like it, but that may be as far as we ever get in using music to help us control or change our emotions.

Through the course of my work with many different types of people who are exhibiting the gamut of emotions, I have come to identify five areas in which music regularly helps a person change their emotional state.

Music can help people:

- focus and distract
- connect and celebrate
- motivate and relax
- evoke memories and enhance new experiences
- tap into our feelings and entertain

The key is to choose music with intention, with a purpose. In order to do that, it is important to step back and identify where you are in a given moment emotionally, and if it's not the right state, then you need to decide where you want to be. When you've identified the end point, then you can best use music to help you.

For herein lies the goal for using music intentionally: that we stop just letting music happen to us and that we begin to choose our music for a specific purpose. Music makes things possible because of what music can do to us at a deep level.

> *To use music with intention is to tune into music's full potential.*

Music Can Focus and Distract

Throughout our day, no matter what we do in life, we're always required to focus our attention on some task or another. Sometimes, in order to focus on what's at hand, it can be very helpful to have distractions. Have you ever watched a college or high-school student study? Many have their ear-buds in and are listening to music. When asked, these students often suggest that music helps them focus because the music distracts the mind from other noises and thus keeps their attention on what they're supposed to be doing.

The technique of using music as distraction to focus better is not ground-breaking. Many have used music to get through boring work or to channel creativity for a specific task. Music can focus us on a task by relaxing our mind and allowing us to feel the work is more manageable.[5] Music in this way distracts us from other things that could be getting in our way.

We all know that music can make routine chores more bearable and many runners who listen to music feel they are going faster and with greater ease. However, there is some research that indicates that acquiring new information is best done with the music off.[6] Nick Perham suggests that the playing of music may work best if you listen to it before working on a task. Then there is the information coming out of the International Conference on Traffic and Transport Psychology. They report that singing along with music in a car may slow a driver's response to potential hazards whereas listening to classical or instrumental music has been found to enhance mental performance.

That may work for some, but I also know plenty of people who find certain kinds of music an important key to concentration. I know of a teenager who listens to Bach while he studies because he feels classical music compared to any other genre and Bach compared to another composer gives him a greater capacity to concentrate. Music distracts him from what's going on outside and helps keep him focused on the task in front of him. He never listens to Bach except when he studies. Through trial and error he figured out for himself that Bach is what worked best. What all this information indicates is how important personal preferences really are.

John: Alone and Needing Something New to Focus On

For those faced with a difficult life circumstance, music provides the needed space to help that person focus—maybe focus on something else so that they relax, or focus their mind on the issue at hand. By using music to focus, oftentimes the person can find some clarity about their situation. I was reminded of how music can clarify in this way when I was referred to a patient in the mental health inpatient unit at the local hospital. As one would expect, I went to the unit anticipating I would be working with someone coping with depression or psychosis. What I didn't expect was a six-foot tall eighteen-year-old boy who looked scared. When I arrived he was curled up in his bed; I was told he had autism.

Before entering his room the staff gave me a brief description of what they were experiencing: physical outbursts such as banging on walls, no verbal communication, and many obsessive behaviours including repetitive spinning and stripping to nakedness. My referral came from the nurse who felt badly that the boy was misplaced in the healthcare system. The unit he was supposed to be in would not have a bed available for another week. When I arrived I found John in a brightly lit, stark white, windowless room with a guard outside his door. I was told the guard was placed there just in case his physical outbursts got out of control.

The guard audibly snickered when he saw my guitar and drum, and said, "Good luck with him," when I entered the room.

John lay in bed with his face to the wall. Because I have worked with many individuals with autism over the years, I knew he most likely was trying to block out the blinding white lights in the room. It was quite over-whelming, even for me. I introduced myself to John. I told him that he didn't have to move and that I was there just to bring some music into the room. I told him he could tell me to stop at any time and that I would immediately go away if he wanted me to.

He didn't move. I began to play a slow lullaby on my guitar gradu-ally adding melody through a hum. His hand came out of the covers and he reached towards me. I let him rest his hand on my strumming wrist and to-gether we strummed the guitar while he remained facing the wall. He began to hum a little and slowly sat up with his eyes tightly squinted. The guard entered; however I shook my head, assuring him that I was fine. The guard kept his hand on the doorknob when John stood up and began to move back and forth.

As his rocking speed increased so did the rhythms of the music. When the lullaby turned into the blues, John started to smile. I incorporated his name into the melody and he increased his eye contact with me immediately while repeating his own name. During thirty minutes of making music together, John calmed down and relaxed. Before I left the room I turned on a CD of music similar to what we had been singing. As I went out the door and looked over my shoulder through the glass window, I watched him continue to rock slightly as he sat on his bed with a smile on his face. The guard looked at me, but didn't say a word.

We don't always have to utilize music dramatically and often. Sometimes the subtle use of music may be more practical to improve the well-being of individuals. At times, it may be more effective to just slow the pace or turn the volume down to create a sense of balance. Often just the slightest change in tempo, volume, pitch, or key can have a tremendous effect, whether the goal is to achieve focus or create distraction.

John just needed music that his body could understand. He responded best to the application of lively, rocking music using variable speeds and volumes. This enabled him to focus on something other than his circumstances—all the new people around and nothing being familiar—distracting him from the rather harsh surroundings that were causing him stress.

As we connect to our music each of us can find the music that our bodies and our minds best respond to, the music that will help us focus on what is important or not important. That focus then can help us achieve any of our desired goals and aspirations.

Music Can Connect and Celebrate

It is easy to feel connected to others when you are listening to music that makes you feel good. People love music for much the same reason they're drawn to sex and delicious food. When you listen to music that moves you, your brain releases dopamine that makes you feel extra good, and when we feel good it becomes easier to feel positive connections to others around us.[7] This information offers a biological explanation for why music has been such a major part of emotional events in cultures around the world since the beginning of human history. When we feel good we connect, and when we get together we celebrate those connections.

Most music is repetitive and, when we find music we like, we tend to play it repeatedly. This helps to stabilize our emotional state by connecting to something that is familiar. New music genres can be investigated by asking friends for suggestions, visiting live music venues, or listening to new radio stations. New music can also help celebrate new beginnings by revealing something about ourselves not there previously. Having a balance of familiar and new music adds texture and spark to the music you listen to daily, something I refer to as your auditory diet which we'll explore further in Part 5.

Heath and Sara: Far Away Loves

For some people, using well-known, repetitive music during a new experience can bring about the desire to connect with others. With their eyes closed, Sarah and Heath leaned back in their chairs listening to the Bach Concerto—a mutual favourite. When the piece ended, it took a few moments for them to open their eyes. On the table in front of each of them, they saw two markers and two sheets of paper. I gently repeated the instructions which I gave them earlier. "I am now going to play the music again. You are each going to draw your own picture. I would like you to both use the two colours you have chosen and draw your relationship in any manner that you choose. Heath, is represented by the blue marker and Sarah is represented by the gold marker, the colours you chose for yourselves earlier."

Sarah smiled at me lovingly, picked up the gold marker, and began drawing before the music started. Heath's deep blue eyes looked at me and with his striking facial features and chiseled jaw, he gave me a silent nod. Sarah and Heath have been married for over forty years and having to be Sarah's caretaker was showing on his face. His beloved wife had late stage Alzheimer's disease.

The Bach concerto started again. During the next several minutes Sarah and Heath worked quietly side by side with Sarah randomly colouring gold all over her circle. Heath spent the first half of the song closing his eyes again and then during the last half he slowly drew two parallel lines down the middle of the page, one in blue and one in gold. The blue line was wavy and the gold line was straight.

When the song finished for the second time, we sat in silence for a few minutes. I turned to Sarah who was still smiling when she looked at me and I asked her about her drawing. She traced her finger over the lines and circles she had made and smiled yet again. I touched her other hand and said, "It really is lovely. Gold suits you." She smiled even more broadly.

I then asked the same question of Heath. "Heath, tell me a little bit about your drawing."

"Well there is not much more to say. This is Sarah (pointing to the straight, gold line) and this is me (pointing to the wavy blue line)."

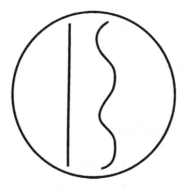

"I keep trying to get close, back to the middle of where we were, but she never moves in completely to meet me, to touch me. She just stays where she is. It will never be the same and I have accepted that. My job now is to make sure she is safe and happy. That's it." Heath's face looked pained.

I then turned to Sarah and asked her what music she liked. With clarity she said, "I love it when he whistles around the house," and pointed to Heath. Heath reached out and gave her a kiss on the back of her hand.

He was still looking at Sarah when he said with a smile, "Oh, I am just making those tunes up, they are nothing special."

She kept looking straight at me and said, "I still like it."

With dementia, repetition is important. Heath can use music re-petitively to help him feel connected with Sarah and celebrate their lives—what they had when she was fully aware and what they have now.[8] Howev-er, for Sarah, improvisational whistling of new, unfamiliar music also had some benefits. His personal music connected him to her. The made up-tunes caught Sarah's attention, but the tone of his voice is what associated her to the man she loved.

Music we associate with our loved one allows us to feel connected to them at all times. I've talked about this phenomenon in part one—that connecting and celebrating are perhaps the two most frequent outcomes I've witnessed with music. There are infinite ways to use music in this way and there is no one way to do it.

What is important is to become more aware of what makes you or someone you love connect to a certain kind of music, and then note that connection. Ask yourself or the person you're trying to connect with what kind of music makes them feel good, or happy, or soothed, or jazzed up. Then explore how that music can help both of you feel more connected—to many things: to each other, to the feeling you want to have but might be alluding you otherwise, to the motivation to get started or to complete the activity you want to accomplish.

Music Can Relax and Motivate

Music is the perfect call to action. It invites you into the main auditorium when you are at a conference, or generates excitement as you recognize the upcoming television show by its theme song, or signifies the next activity when you are at the gym. In the book The Power of Music, Elena Mannes highlights how music affects different groups of people.[9] For example infants seem to prefer smooth-sounding tones and have adverse reactions to dissonant, jarring sounds. In addition to helping people feel soothed, music can also stimulate more parts of the brain than any other human function or activity. That's why music holds tremendous capacity to change the brain and affect the way it works.

In 1959 a doctor named Teirich undertook one of the earliest studies into the therapeutic effects of music and vibration.[10] He built a couch which contained loud speakers and which transferred vibration from J.S. Bach's D minor Toccata and Fugue straight to the solar plexus. He used his fellow doctors as a subject group. They variously reported immediate warmth in the solar plexus, a feeling of complete relaxation in the stomach along with a burst of optimism.

Music can get you excited while waiting in anticipation, and can make you feel like you can work out a little longer and harder. A friend of mine loves to put on Aretha Franklin or Ray Charles when she's cleaning the house. She sings along, feels relaxed, productive, and motivated all at the same time.

Rick: Goes to Scarborough Fair

This juxtaposition of motivation and relaxation was never more startling to me than one day at the local hospital. I have an on-going music therapy group there, and on my scheduled day, I went to facilitate my group.

Walking towards my therapy room, I passed by Rick who paced the same twenty-metre hall he had walked for the past several weeks. He never seemed to get tired of the same strip of floor at the hospital and would move at a fairly good clip from the nurse's station to the doors of the group room at the end of the hall. He was a very tall man with intense blue eyes, a long unruly dirty blond beard, and wore one or two hats depending on his mood. Rick was admitted to the hospital a number of times.

When not in the hospital, Rick did his best to collect bottles around the city streets and live from shelter to shelter. He had no family and due to the severity of his mental illness struggled to hold on to any job. When he would become too sick to look after himself he would oftentimes be picked up by police officers and taken to the hospital. Although physically imposing, he was known by staff and residents as "the gentle giant." Before this particular day, I had actually never heard his voice even though I had seen him many times before.

As I entered the unit with my guitar, I called out a casual, "Hello, Rick." He continued to walk with purpose and, as I had come to expect, gave me no response. I continued down the hall and went into the group room to introduce myself to the seven women who waited for me. They were all admitted to the hospital and were members of what was known as "the depression group." One woman in her early twenties and eight months pregnant looked nervous sitting quietly in a chair.

A fifty-five-year old revealed that she had lost her husband in an inexplicable car accident several months earlier and couldn't seem to cry. Three woman pronounced their lives to be complicated—it was impossible to get through with all of the expectations and obligations they had to meet on a day-to-day basis. One mom had overcome breast cancer and could not figure out how to fit into her old world. The last woman, Melissa, whom I knew from previous sessions, could no longer count how many visits she had made to the hospital. Melissa had difficulty with people who got too close to her.

As usual, she found a spot on the edge of a couch, and gently asked that no one sit too close. Unlike Rick, these women had chosen to be here on their quest to find the happiness that continued to elude them.

We sat in a circle and considered what music in our lives could be used best to achieve moments of being "less sad." Melissa reflected on the music she listened to when she felt in "better spirits."

"Could we try singing some of that music now?" I asked.

"Sure, why not."

We began to sing when Rick unexpectedly burst through the doors of our private room. We all jumped a little and then one woman closest to him said, "Oh, Hi Rick, we are having a private group." He looked at me. Within a millisecond his eyes changed from intense to soft, and he seemed to be in awe at the sight of the guitar on my lap. He looked around the room, saw the vacant spot next to Melissa, and sat down. Melissa moved closer to the edge of the couch looking nervous but she smiled at Rick and said hello.

Rick stretched out his long legs, leaned back on the couch, put his hands behind his head, looked at me, and then he began to sing in a deep baritone voice:

"Are you goin' to Scarbourough Fair?"

Without cuing, the woman joined in sweetly with "Parsley, sage, rosemary and thyme." The women also visibly relaxed by the time they reached the next phrase of the song. I picked up my guitar and strummed along with the familiar phrases, "remember me to one who lives there, she once was a true love of mine."

Together we sang through two verses of the Simon and Garfunkel classic following Rick's stunningly warm singing voice coupled with the women's pretty tones. Rick stopped singing and turned to Melissa to give her a warm, handsome smile and said "that was great, thank you."

He then turned to me and said, "What's next?" The ladies agreed that it would be okay if Rick stayed with them and they could all sing their favourite songs. We did just that.

At the end of the group session, Rick stood up and left the room. That was the last time I saw him as he was being transferred to a long-term care facility in another town. As the door closed behind him, the women looked at each other, began to smile, and then laughed. The most striking transformation was in the young woman who was pregnant. She was so much more relaxed, and I rejoiced inside as I watched her laughing with the others.

Later that day Melissa said to me, "The music helped me today. It was so nice when Rick joined us. For a moment, we all felt normal. I haven't felt that way in a long time."

The most startling surprise was with Rick. Music motivated the gentle giant to stop pacing and join a group, entering a new environment he had not previously experienced. This not only helped him in that moment, but the music we made that day relaxed the other group members into a state of feeling more "normal." If music was able to relax such a diverse group of individuals, suffering with day-to-day anxieties and stress, serious enough that they were needing hospital support, just imagine how one of your stressful days could be turned around.[11]

Music Can Evoke Memories and Enhance New Experiences

Music is well-known to hold important influence on our memories. We associate songs with emotions, people, and places we have experienced in the past. I've always found it interesting that when songs are played for a client, the clients generally have more memories associated with songs that they consider "pleasing" than are evoked by "non-pleasing" songs.

But do the pleasing songs evoke the memories, or do we like the songs because we associate them with memories? For a person who sustains a head injury, accessing these memories in just the right way can soothe the person as well as inviting him or her into a new experience they otherwise may not have had.

The primary consideration of a Music Therapist when dealing with a head injury is to address all aspects of the person sitting in front of them:

1. *Who they were* - what was important to them prior to their injury and how can the music of their past access their best (happy, productive, important) memories. Then using these music-based anchors support the individual's ongoing rehabilitation.

2. ***Who they are*** - what do they need right now and how can music make them feel successful and motivated to continue their healing journey. When used intentionally to do so, music therapy can improve the many injuries that may result from brain trauma including impairment of speech and language processing, impairment of physical abilities, impairment of cognitive processing, loss or disorganization of memory and emotional distress. There have been tremendous results in speech rehabilitation using a technique known as melodic intonation therapy.[12]

3. ***Who they desire to become*** - what do they hope to achieve and how can music help them get there. Writing new music, songs of hopes and desires, can be a fresh experience that brings to light the future and that change is on the horizon.

Wayne: Takes it Easy

I had been working with Wayne for six months. He was in his late forties and had sustained a head injury at work that left him unable to communicate. His youngest daughter sat beside him daily and let staff know his likes and dislikes. She told me that Wayne loved music, all kinds of music but mostly rock and roll from the seventies and eighties.

In the spring that year, I received a call informing me that Don Felder, formerly of the Eagles, would be visiting our city and that he wanted to do a fundraiser for music therapy.[13] He also wanted an opportunity to visit people who were coping with unique challenges and who used music to inspire them. I immediately thought of Wayne and worked it out that Don would visit him.

The staff anxiously waited to see what the response from Wayne would be. When Don arrived, he introduced himself, "Hi, my name is Don, for twenty years I played with a group you might remember—the Eagles."

Wayne's eyes dilated as he lifted his head. Don put his guitar on his lap, strummed two measures, and began to sing:

"Well I was runnin' down the road trying to loosen my load,
I got seven women on my mind,
four that want to own me,

two that want to scold me,
one says she's a friend of mine."

I saw Wayne lift his head and hold it there, a movement that seemed difficult for him in the past as he could barely do it for more than three or four minutes. For Don, Wayne held up his head for song after song after song. He listened to Don's stories with a twinkle in his eye that was absent in the past. Don's last song was his renowned "Hotel California." He welcomed everyone to join in. We sang, we cried, and we had goose-bumps down to our toes. Wayne didn't release his warm grin. He looked at his daughter, and I swear I saw a wink.

While we'll never know what Wayne was remembering as he listened to the Eagles' songs, I do know this—the music of his youth brought him back to those carefree teen years when everything new carries with it an element of excitement. As we visit with friends, travel to new locations, experiment with feelings of love and longing, music is often not too far away. Experiences are anchored in our music memory, and we draw on them over and over as we move into our middle and advanced years. For Wayne those memories may have been from his distant past, but when he heard the music later in his life, and in this case exactly the way he heard it the first time, with the voice he was most familiar with, he was able to accomplish something he couldn't previously do.

Music Can Tune into Feelings and Entertain

Music can bring life to many moments. It supports our enjoyment of the events in our day. Some people believe that music was important to human evolution, from how we develop language to how we pass down information to new generations.[14] And because we respond well to repetition, our brains are constantly predicting what is coming up next based on the music pattern. This is how we find ourselves naturally tapping our toes, dancing, and generally being entertained by the sounds we hear. Even in times of sadness, people can feel love and even find laughter.

Harry: The Christmas Letter

It was just before Christmas when Harry invited me to spend an evening with him and his family. When he suggested I come to his home to facilitate a music-filled evening he included a very compelling reason. "It is the first time in ten years that all my children will be home for Christmas, and I want to make it special for them."

He went on to say, "You said that by giving people a choice of song, you are giving every person a voice and an opportunity to teach you something about themselves. I want to hear what is important to my children and create an evening to remember." How could I resist?

It certainly was an evening to remember—full of songs, stories, emotions, and heartfelt family spirit. Music, the master connector, was at work again helping people be entertained all the while helping everyone present tap into their feelings about the people around them and the experiences they shared.

A month later I received a letter from Harry.

Dear Jennifer,

I can't thank you enough for coming to my home at Christmas time. It was the "special time" I knew it would be. What I didn't mention to you then is that I have experiencing extreme and unusual mood swings. These changes in behaviour have been very difficult and frustrating for my family. They have been very worried. Just shortly after Christmas I was given the diagnosis I was expecting. I have Alzheimer's Disease. Last Christmas may be my last Christmas I remember with my family. I hope the music will trigger the special memories we shared that evening.

Thank you for the gift of music. Harry

Harry was exactly correct—music, when used with the right intention has the power to take you from feeling totally lost to feeling more comfortable and less alone. In a brief moment, music can take you from feeling unruly to calm. For Harry, the use of Christmas music around the Christmas season will continue to trigger associations to being with his family and the deeper feelings that go along with these associations.

Although Harry hired me under the guise of entertaining his family over the Christmas holidays his reasons were much more purposeful— to bridge his memories and feelings to the evening so he can remember later. More than just entertainment, music is a path to healing and compassion, to connecting to our feelings, our environment and the people around us—to feel connected to a bigger experience, a memory, and a person we love.

However, music doesn't always have to be associated with saying goodbye (even though I'm sure most of you can remember the music you turned to when someone broke your heart.) Music can evoke the gamut of memories—from the songs you sang as a child, to riding around in your car when you were a teenager and didn't have a care in the world except maybe worrying about how you looked in your jeans. How many of your most important life experiences have music associated with them?

I'm sure plenty.

The whole point here is actually quite simple. We already use music to either enhance or change our emotional state. From going to a concert to Christmas music at home, listening to music helps you connect to your emotions. The aim is to do so consciously.

Listening to music can also revive feelings that we have associated with that music almost instantly. Some of those feelings may not be ideal—and we're going to deal with music and emotional triggers in the next part of the book. But for now, I want you to think about something. People with dementia and brain injury can become calmer or access memories and feelings just by listening to music. If music is that powerful for people who's minds have been compromised by disease or by trauma, what do you think music can do for you?

How many more ways can we change our emotional state for the better simply by using the right music as a focus?

The Value of Silence

Music is a complex and intricate blend of sound and silence. Dr. Helen Lees, author of Silence in our Schools, notes that there is "a natural silence for people to Tune into, to develop, to come towards, that is helpful for living and learning, developing and understanding, interacting and knowing. Silence brings peace, healing, joy, simplicity, and truth. It brings about the laying of foundations of understanding." In her book, she likens silence to oil, something that needs to be sourced and mined in order to capture its power of transformation. Silence, like oil, is one of life's greatest commodities.[15]

I first experienced true silence during an all-day cross-country ski trip. Being at the back of the pack and knowing I was not in top shape, I made sure to pace myself. Occasionally, I stopped after a particularly difficult hill and pretended to adjust my boots, or take off my gloves when in fact I was catching my breath.

During one of those stops, the group in front of me disappeared around a bend in the trail, and suddenly I felt a blast of silence. There was no sound or transfer of vibration or wind in my ears. It made me stop and immediately brought my whole being into clear focus. I felt a reverence for all that was around me, and I made sure not to turn too fast, knowing this feeling would end.

I was not scared. Soothed by silence's embrace, I felt almost hugged by nature as I heard it telling me, "Here is your moment, enjoy."

"Jennifer are you okay back there?" My friend called back to me. The moment was over. I was sorry to have to respond and continued on our trek. Never before had I experienced silence in such a powerful way.

In speech, it is in a moment of silence that one also fully appreciates the intentionality of what has been said. The listener understands that he is being singled out and "spoken to." Silence provides a pocket of space in which the sound just heard can be processed and consciously responded to. It is the listener's opportunity to react and give something in return. Silence can also be used to create anticipation for what comes next.

Music uses silence in the same way—to capture your attention, to lure, to grab hold, to hug, to suspend the listener through a silent pause. It ensures you escape from sound, leaving room for an even greater impact the next time. By giving you the space you need, it propagates the energy of the music and leaves you hungry, desiring more.

Exercise: Breathe

Because music is that intricate blend of sound and silence, what many don't realize is how comforting the very sound of our breathing can be. If you are feeling overwhelmed, or perhaps feeling extra sensitive to sensory stimulation—if just leaving the house in the morning can feel like a challenge here is a short exercise to use.

Breathe.

That's it.

The research is clear that three deep breaths can reduce your fight or flight response.[16] By breathing more deeply you can break the cycle of panic. Breathing exercises can help reduce tension and relieve stress, thanks to an extra boost of oxygen. While shallow breathing, a marker of stress, stimulates the sympathetic nervous system, deep breathing does the opposite and helps us to calm down.

What's more, breathing exercises have been proven to support the systems that can be harmed by stress. A moment of silence with just deep breathing can reduce blood pressure and may even be able to change the expression of some genes.

Everybody has an overwhelm point. It is different for everyone. Many of us just keep pushing through the stress but our goals of accomplishment and productivity become much harder to achieve in this state. With the simple act of three deep breathes anywhere you are, you are combating those stress responses and putting your body in a healthier place to better cope with whatever is to come.

CHAPTER 3

Triggers and Anchors

These days, there is more rhythm in our lives than harmony.
Jeff Clayton, to Wayne Shorter

The ability to perceive emotion in music develops early in childhood, and changes throughout development.[1] Just as different people perceive events differently based upon their past experiences, emotions elicited by listening to different types of music are affected due to previous experiences that are often intensely personal.[2] While some studies indicate that music training is correlated with high music intelligence as well as higher IQ, other studies refute the claim.[3,4] However what is worth noting is that exposure to music earlier in life seems to affect behavioral choices, schoolwork, and social interactions later in life.[5]

Throughout our life the world presents us with a variety of sounds. Doors slamming, dogs barking, radios playing in the background. We're so used to most of those sounds that we don't even realize that they're there until they startle us or annoy us. But if the world suddenly went soundless, I suspect we would feel and hear a great loss. Not only would sound disappear but so would the vibrations that help guide us—the feelings under our feet as music plays, the auditory cues of when we are in a safe verses unsafe setting as defined by the different sounds that we hear.

Up to this point, we have talked about music more in general terms, about how, when we shift our viewpoint just slightly from just being a passive listener of music to a more intentionally active user, the potential for us to do better and feel better in life can improve drastically.

Part 3 definitely follows the trend of how to use music intentionally, but now we're going to talk about one of the more specific aspects of music that is critical to understand if we are to maximize our music.

It's all about triggers. To many the word has negative connotations. Whatever "triggers" us makes us "go off "—as the word implies. You smell tequila and it makes your stomach churn because when you were young and foolish in college, you drank too many tequila shooters and it made you sick. Just like our sense of smell, music can trigger all sorts of responses in a person. Most think about negative triggers, but I want to suggest to you that part of the power of music is this: if music is so powerful that it can trigger us negatively, then it can trigger us "happy" too. By being more aware of what your music or "auditory" triggers are, you can use them proactively to help you create a more positive, upbeat environment for yourself, one that is less stressful, more relaxing or energizing, depending on what you need in that moment in time.

Auditory triggers are sounds, songs or styles of music that quickly evoke an emotional state.

As we have identified, stress contributes to many human diseases.[6] Particular types of stress are the biggest factors in people feeling low or even depressed. Social stressors such as divorce and the death of a loved one are some of the worst culprits. However, there are also the broad-spectrum stressors of grief and loss: loss of control, loss of a job, the loss of a relationship or even grieving missed opportunities.

Brad was affected by the loss of his independent life. Donna was grieving the loss of her dad, leading to increased stress on her and her family, compounded by feelings of guilt while making the difficult decision to put her dad in a care centre. For both cases music became a trigger to something better—an improved state of mind and an opportunity to express their values in a real way.

Daily workplace stress continues to manifest in our society leading to all sorts of residual problems such as dissatisfied relationships, lack of productivity, a general air of disappointment, and the more serious medical conditions that many struggle with.

I propose that music is a wonderful auditory trigger to cope with stress simply, quickly, and at minimal cost.

Because auditory triggers are very effective in helping a person deal with the stress of life, it is important to understand the two ways in which auditory triggers are created. Both are premised on the person having no previous association with a piece of music:

Inspired Music Trigger - this is the type of trigger that happens when you hear a piece of music that you haven't had a previous relationship to, but strong feelings arise from it independent of anything that may be happening. This also creates an association that you can then trigger at a later point in time to recreate the feelings you first had when you first heard that piece of music.

When a piece of music affects you, a trigger exists. And knowing what music affects you can lead you to make better choices in determining what music to listen to:

I hear music

I feel something

Later I want to feel that way again

I play the music

The music triggers those same feelings

Associated Music Trigger - an associated trigger can be created when you have strong feelings caused by an event at a time when you hear a piece of music. At that time your brain will associate that piece of music with those strong feelings which gives you the ability to trigger those same feelings later when you play that same piece of music.

Music plays

Something happens

The music is associated
with the event

Later I hear the same music

The music triggers the
same association

While you can sometimes consciously choose your music triggers, most of the time the correlation between the music and the connected event are purely coincidental. This is especially true for negative triggers.

James: The Long and Winding Road - When a Trigger Fires

As my family got into the rental van to leave on a four hour drive to our vacation destination, I felt confident that we had everything packed. I spent the past few weeks booking the place we were going to stay, planning our dog's vacation at the sitter's, setting the menus, and purchasing the right amount of food to feed our two teenagers and their two teenaged friends for a week. I suggested the right clothing items, informed the friends' parents about our itinerary, and identified how we would pack everything and everyone without having to resort to a roof rack.

On departure day, I happily jumped into the passenger seat and looked behind me at four happy, excited faces. Our things packed neatly and perfectly situated so James, my husband, could see well out the back window without any obstructions. There is nothing quite as satisfying as a well-executed road trip. That is, until someone or something dampens the perfection.

We have a rule in our family—the driver is in charge of choosing the music for the duration of the driving time. Prior to the trip, I didn't give this much thought as I am typically in control of the car. The music for this long drive, however, was under the control of my husband who was excited to be at the helm. He had grown up taking many long family road trips and like myself was looking forward to the whole experience.

With the music on, we all happily pulled out of the driveway. We were only eight minutes outside of city limits when I was shocked into reality. We were listening to the fourth track on the same album we had started with when we left the driveway. Could this be happening? Was it possible we were going to listen to the entire extended edition of Supertramp's Crime of the Century album. Worse, was I not to be consulted?

After about the fifth song, I felt my pulse begin to rise and a mild agitation start in the pit of my stomach. Initially, I told myself that I was being foolish. I like a couple of Supertramp songs. But when that fifth track started, I knew I had passed the threshold. My trigger had fired and I was totally ticked off. This is a perfect example of a negatively inspired music trigger.

I tried concentrating on browsing my smart phone and contemplated updating my facebook status regarding my growing music misery.[7] I knew some of my friends would say I was crazy! Knowing the rules, I sunk down in the seat. I knew I had no voice—the driver was in control. James had what I am sure was a slight smirk on his face but not once took his eyes off the road. How could he let it bother me and not change the music? After five Supertramp songs James stopped moving his head and tapping on the steering wheel. Turning towards me he casually asked, "Hey would you like to listen to something else?"

I started to laugh. "Is it that obvious?" At that point I realized that my hands were clenched tight and I had been leaning towards the door, obviously desperately trying to escape.

If you knew James, you would not be surprised to learn that we spent the next two hours debating the "right" driving music. His point of view was that to truly appreciate great music you must listen to the album from beginning to the end. Furthermore, the best way to listen correctly to the music was on a long drive, such as this rare occasion. For me, long drives should be accompanied by a mixed playlist that would appeal to the masses and encourage group sing-a-longs.[8]

James and I are only twenty-four hours apart in age, married for almost twenty years, grew up in similar family settings with similar experiences and knew the same music. Our music taste for car trips could not be more different.

So, as we listened to James' choice of music, I felt a huge surge of negative emotion. But clenching my fists and trying to escape were only the tip of the iceberg. Because I had been triggered negatively, James' actions changed my whole persona. I convinced myself in the span of twenty minutes or so that my once wonderful husband was self-centred and thoughtless.

If a person is having a negative response to the music being played, they will often transfer those feelings to the relationships around them. I mirrored that in my response to James in the car.

Fortunately, James realized my strong emotional response was misplaced and I, in turn, was missing out on an important music experience, and we were able to process the issues involved and we resolved our differences on appropriate driving music.

Although Supertramp was a negative trigger in this context, if my personal music preferences were played those music triggers would have affected me in a completely opposite way. James was in music heaven listening to some of his favorite songs. He was feeling relaxed and was definitely joyful. He was experiencing positive triggers. It made me wonder—how easy would it be to help others when not everyone is triggered by the same music? Although at times difficult, it is possible.

Since getting triggered can happen to everyone, it is crucial to understand how the process works so we can be more gentle on ourselves and others. The trigger elicits an emotional response. Our brain, which is really our computer, processes the emotion through our bodies. It tells the body to release chemicals such as endorphins if it's good and adrenaline if it's bad. Our brains have been perfectly designed to support and sustain our survival in this way. Our emotions are critical because they are an instant feedback loop about whether a person, experience, or the environment is positive or negative, safe or a threat, something to move towards or away. These responses to our emotions is in the ancient of the brain called the limbic system. A key structure in this area is the amygdala. The amygdala is always in the background waiting to take over our emotions when required to do so.

When we see or hear something that triggers the feeling of threat, the amygdala comes forward instantaneously, and we act before we have time to think. That part of us that reasons in our mind takes a back seat to the reactive part, and the brain responds by relegating the pre-frontal cortex or reasoning part of our brain to the back seat so we can protect ourselves from the threat and ultimately preserve our life as it is. Dan Goleman, in his bestseller Emotional Intelligence, calls this action "an amygdala highjacking." [9]

The emotional response to a selection of music, how music is administered, and the frequency of music has an effect on each of us. It is therefore important to be aware of our personal triggers to music and to remember that other people are just as easily triggered. This includes sounds, the volume that music is played at, and even silence.

The Boys: Harsh Confinement

Sometimes I'm struck by how profound these triggers can be. I was once contacted by a psychologist: "We would like you to facilitate a three-hour session with a group of boys who have committed the most serious of crimes, and a few of them are to be incarcerated for more than a year."

The boys were entering a twelve-week substance abuse program. The staff realized it would take three to four weeks for the boys to establish themselves into one cohesive group where they could function well together. The staff desperately needed to maximize the program and hoped music would speed up the process in uniting the boys before their next rehabilitation program commenced.

"The boys range in age from thirteen to eighteen," she said "and there will be eight of them. You will be the only staff in the room, but don't worry—it is a glass room and officers will be watching everything that is happening." I felt nervous energy in the pit of my stomach, and internally questioned my ability to manage this project. With a confident tone, I stated, "That sounds great. I'll see you in July!"

I worked endlessly planning the three-hour session which was by far my longest workshop in such an intimate setting. I remembered when I was a teenager how quickly I assessed the adult authorities in my life. It would take all of thirty seconds for me to conclude whether I liked the person or not and how much investment I would make in our relationship. I was sure my new clients had a similar timeline and wondered if I could establish a strong relationship in thirty seconds.

The Young Offenders Centre was at the far edge of town.[10] I had not been to this district before and was told to take the fourth driveway to the right. I saw the first driveway and continued down the winding road past two maximum security facilities and endless steel fences with barbed wire at the top. I was struck by the remoteness of the area—no-one visible and total silence. I was the only car on the road, and I felt myself getting nervous again.

After three security check stops, I left my personal belongings in a locked case and headed to the last check stop. I finally made it to my square visiting room with wall-to-wall glass. The officers told me to set up whatever I needed and I would have ten minutes before the boys arrived. With my brain working on overtime, I imagined goatees, tattoos, and stern faces.

The clean-shaven boys who entered were younger than I imagined, wearing matching orange track suits. Some were probably not even old enough to shave. One or two smiled a sweet smile as they looked at the instruments. Each boy sat around the table with a pad of paper and a pen in front of them. They looked at me expectantly.

I opened with, "I had the hardest time coming up with what to do with you first. Music has been such an important part of my life, but I have no idea whether it is important to you. I would love to know what role music has played in your life so far."

Rob spoke first, "My dad used to play Bruce Springsteen in the basement. I used to like hanging out on the couch listening to the music with him. He played it nice and loud."

I heard many more stories of singing with dads, singing with moms, hanging out with friends, and singing TV theme songs. We talked about music—not so much about different kinds of music or even about the music they liked, but about the relationships and memories that connected them to their past. When the discussion came to a close, I stood up and went over to the white board. It was only then that I remembered officers were watching from the outside. I waved to them. The boys imitated me and waved as well.

On the big white board, I made a graph with three columns across and four rows down. At the top of the columns I wrote "Feeling," "Inside," and "Outside."

I pointed to the word "Feeling" and asked, "As a group, let's come up with three primary feelings we experience every day. Then we are going to list the sounds from inside this centre that make us feel that way. Then we are going to list the sounds from outside this centre that make us feel that way."

Rob started by saying the word "harsh." The rest of the boys nodded and laughed. They high-fived each other at how clever they had been to come up with that word. I carefully wrote down the word HARSH in capital letters under the "Feeling" column.

As I pointed to the space beside the word HARSH and under the word INSIDE I asked, "What sound, when you hear it, evokes a 'harsh' feeling."

The boys became silent, and I worried they didn't understand the question. Rob whispered to the boy beside him and I saw a few nods. He leaned forward a little, looked at me, and said something that sounded like "pssstoop." The boy next to him nodded knowingly and said the same word. Finally, all the boys were saying the word repeatedly, until it almost sounded like a rap. Even though I thought they were yanking my chain because I didn't recognize the sound, I turned around and wrote the word "pssstoop." I knew I had to find out more and asked, "Would someone please tell me where you hear this sound?"

Rob stopped rapping and with a serious tone said, "Well ma'am, that is the sound of the doors air-locking us in at night." I nodded with a new understanding and we moved on to the rest of the activity.

When the woman in my running group asked me to "shush," I felt humiliated even though it was many years since I had last heard it. This was my personal "trigger." My guess is that years later, the sound of "pssstoop" may make those boys, who would now be grown, have memories of something harsh.

The research supports this idea of triggers. People report feeling certain emotions when listening to music and these emotions are not always the same to those sitting next to them. In one study researchers presented excerpts of fast tempo, major mode music and slow tempo, and minor mode music to participants. These musical structures were chosen because they have been proven to convey happiness and sadness respectively. Participants indicated higher rankings of happiness after listening to music with tones that convey happiness and elevated rankings of sadness after music with sad tones. This evidence suggests that notes used to express emotions in music can also elicit those same emotions in the listener.[11]

I have interviewed many individuals about why they listen to music that the majority of society perceives as sad and the answers are usually based on validation. By using music that feels sad to them, other feelings such as isolation are not felt; in other words, they don't feel alone. Other reasons people give for listening to sad music is to retrieve memories or to feel closer to other people. What is most intriguing, however, is when sad music actually makes a person feel happier. The sad music strikes a vibrational harmony with the person's emotional tone, and that can lift them up, even just a little.

While it is important to recognize which sounds create negative emotions, I am on a personal mission to help people recognize the positive sounds in their lives. During the same activity with the boys, we were able to explore some of the sounds that exuded happiness. These familiar sounds and music from home gave them feelings of hope of being able to experience those sounds again. Sounds around family gatherings, meeting friends, and going to dances musically triggered a sense of happiness and something to look forward to.

Whether you are choosing music for the car or for the workplace, suggesting music to help others relax, or wondering if you are going to put up those bamboo chimes on your porch this summer, remember that people are easily triggered by music, sound and silence—for better or worse. To use music intentionally is to recognize which sounds are triggering negative and positive emotions, and then finding ways to reduce the incidence of the negative sounds, and to increase the incidence of positive sounds, in the end creating an environment that makes people feel just good being there.

Kate: On the Ocean of Life

Kate lived by her herself in a dark, cramped, single-bedroom basement apartment.

Every morning, Kate used the support that had been attached from the side of her bed to the ceiling to pull herself up, swing her legs to one side, and sit on the edge of her mattress. Then she used all her remaining strength to heave herself into the wheelchair next to her bed.

Next she would have to maneuver her large frame chair through the various nooks and crannies of her small apartment to complete her morning routine of going to the bathroom, brushing her teeth, making herself breakfast and checking her messages.

I knocked on her door every Wednesday and was welcomed with a cheerful, "Come in." As I entered, I heard the now expected, "Sorry for the mess." I took a few moments to help her clear off the breakfast dishes at the table where she was sitting. I set up the instruments I had brought, placing them near her keyboard, lowering the table a little so she could lean in and see everything.

"How are you doing today, Kate?"

"Not too bad for a shut-in." she said with a twinkle.

I looked up at her beautiful, young, thirty-eight year old face. She struggled with the brake on her wheelchair as her fingers were no longer able to move the way they once did. She was attempting to use the heel of her hand to get it into place.

Kate was first diagnosed with Multiple Sclerosis (MS) ten years earlier. When we first met, she described her disease to me. She said, "Multiple Sclerosis is like a body snatcher leaving only your mind and a carcass to lug around."

You would not recognize any grief or loss at first glance, as Kate takes extra care in her appearance, presenting herself as a strong person full of assurance, regardless of her disability. She would describe herself as a teacher by trade with the heart of a poet who loves to philosophize and remain a student of life. Her favourite leisure activities include listening and participating in making music and writing poetry.

When she could no longer continue her career as a teacher she began to explore new opportunities, one of which was an evening group guitar class that I was leading. Kate felt that learning the guitar might lessen the deterioration she was feeling. It is easy to remember that particular guitar class as it was full of laughter and fun. It was a group of thirty to fifty year olds learning guitar for the first time. They relished the learning of music and thoroughly enjoyed re-living their high school years. By the end of the class they performed "House of the Rising Sun," "Blowing in the Wind," and "Brown–Eyed Girl" —all in unison. What they lacked in guitar skills they made up for in vocal enthusiasm, often singing above the sounds of a missed or altered chord. Kate was still walking at that point and would slowly carry her guitar into the room each week.

Today, Kate started by selecting one of her favourite pieces from her personal soundtrack—songs that were important to her at different stages in her life. It took us several weeks to compile the list, and it was a highly emotional experience. (I will delve into more depth on how to create your own personal soundtrack in part 4.) Some of the stories accompanying the songs were humorous, some heartbreaking, and all were layered with strong emotional memories.

After we discussed the instruments I had displayed on the table, Kate picked up her mallet, gave me a quick smile and a wink, and focused again on the table. When she was ready, she hit the right note on a chime. The sound resonated in the air. She struck another instrument made of wood and then the drum. Slowly each sound reverberated through her tiny ground floor apartment. As she gained momentum, she nodded slightly, indicating that it was time for me to join her. I responded and matched her rhythms and several minutes later accompanied her on the keyboard.

Her music creation continued without words, only tones, sounds, and the occasional wink and smile. Thirty minutes later we were finished. She placed the mallet back on the table. Without turning towards me she said, "It is amazing that how I am feeling today was reflected in the music we created together. I feel whole. Although I feel troubled because of what I have lost, I still love life. How can I have MS and still find happiness? People think I am crazy."

Her face glowed as she spoke. We talked about the positive energy she was able to muster as she coped through something so difficult. As in all sessions, she ended by writing an impromptu poem that would later be put to music. Her song for that day went like this:

I'm on the ocean of life.
I see the depths to freedom Realizing where I am
And what I am here for.
I am a vessel of truth.

Kate revealed that writing and memorizing lyrics to her own pieces had been extremely healing. Music does not affect the MS; it does, however, trigger the positives in her life, helping her to escape from the grief brought on by her ever-changing circumstances.

As we find our music triggers and begin to use them consciously, there is a time of trial and error. Even for me as a trained Music Therapist, I do not always get it right. When a mistake is made, it is important to just stop the music and make an immediate shift in tactic.

Baby: How I Got it All Wrong Blues

When I prepared to deliver my second child, I decided to create background music to calm my mind and ease my perception of pain. I knew about music in the hospital environment but never used music in the labour and delivery unit. A colleague gave me some pointers on putting my music together and over several months, I carefully selected the music that inspired me and evoked a natural relaxation response. I even put them in an order that induced a positive flow.

I practiced by laying on my living room floor, playing the music and feeling comfortably relaxed. I was ready. I was going to breathe in and sing this baby out.

My labour started slowly with the contractions far apart. Suddenly, the repetition increased with a vengeance. "Turn on the music." I yelled to James. He immediately turned on the first song. "Please, change the song," I grunted. He changed it again. The next song started. "Did I pick these songs?" I asked him. They sounded foreign, grating, annoying. Songs that once soothed were now painful. With frustration in the moment I asked James to turn off the music.

I ended up delivering my daughter in utter silence or more accurately, she was bathed in the sound of my husky roar accompanied by power-pushing.

What went wrong? The music was supposed to make the labour and delivery easier? With all the practicing I had done, I had associated my "labour music" with the relaxed state I was in as while on my living room carpet. Those were moments of Pure Zen.

So, what happened? The trigger worked. As the music was playing it was bringing feelings of relaxation and zen, but in the moment of giving birth, that feeling of being relaxed wasn't what I wanted, so I turned off the music. Even the most well-intentioned trained professionals can get it wrong.

As long as humans have communicated with drums and plucked strings, music has provided a sense of well-being by lifting spirits and calming nerves. There is a well-known study among Music Therapists about a neuroscientist who was a patient at his own clinic.[12] As he was being prepped for spinal surgery, he thought of his dentist who often gave patients earphones to help ease their anxiety. The neuroscientist reasoned if root canal patients were using music to release tension then why not use music for brain surgery patients who are typically awake during the lengthy procedure? Furthermore, he reasoned that there could be a breakthrough therapeutic benefit.

After his own surgery, the doctor made a decision to add music to his patient's experience in the operating room in the hope of easing their stress. Brain surgery patients who were wide awake listened to music during their brain operation. With their neural activity recorded, researchers identified how those selections made them feel. The doctor successfully concluded that patients are more relaxed in the operating room if the right music is played.

More than just entertainment and marketing, music is now used for stress relief in dental offices as well as the operating room.

There are a number of studies that show when surgeons—both medical and dental—listen to music in the operating room, they work more effectively. The doctors show physical indicators of being more relaxed, as indicated by measurements of their nervous system activity. However, the study also found that surgeons are not asking others in the operating room for their preferences: one survey of anesthetists found that about a quarter felt that music "reduced their vigilance and impaired their communication with other staff," and about half felt that music was distracting when they were dealing with a problem with the anesthesia.[13]

Like all good intentions, if certain measures are not taken with the implementation, the desired outcomes will be missed.

Doctors: Operating Room Music

Diane was scheduled for day surgery, but her operating room experience didn't quite meet with the expectations of relaxation and tranquility.

Diane was informed she would be placed under general anesthetic. The nurses greeted her when she arrived and assisted her in getting ready for surgery. She was informed that the surgery would last approximately two to three hours and she would wake up feeling sore but refreshed. She was assisted onto the operating table and asked if she was comfortable. She noticed herself taking several deep breaths as she waited for the doctor to arrive. The anesthetist leaned over and asked if they could play music during her surgery because "music helps to relax the patient."

"Like recorded music?'" she asked, "or do you sing as you put me out?"

The anesthetist laughed and said, "No, I think you would prefer recorded music instead of my voice." She was very pleased and said that she thought it would be great. But in the end it wasn't. He turned on a generic radio station without asking Diane's preferences. One song was just coming to an end and another was about to start. By the time Diane closed her eyes she heard the final words of the familiar chorus, "This will be the day that I die." Her last thoughts before going out were, "I certainly hope not!"

While Diane's doctor wanted her to feel safe during the operation and knew the benefits of music, the experience would have been more effective if the doctor would have had just a bit more knowledge about the effects of music. You do not want to have unexpected negative messages, and the words in a song can create those unintended consequences. When we consider triggers it is important to remind ourselves that triggers work in several ways. We can be positively or negatively triggered, and we can positively or negatively trigger others. That's what was going on when James was listening to his music in the car. It worked for him but not for me.

Another example of triggers in action is the typical situation when you are at an intersection and a car pulls up in the next lane interrupting the peaceful sunny afternoon. You feel the vibrations of the bass reverberating through the entire car. A young man wearing sunglasses pulls up beside you in his Mustang convertible, his thumb is banging on the steering wheel, his head is bobbing to the beat. By this time you are definitely annoyed, as evidenced by your furrowed brow. The light changes and he drives off. You drive off slowly to ensure he gets well ahead of you. He is relaxed and excited about the day but your energy levels, on the other hand, have just taken a beating and you need a new jolt.

At that point, you have two choices: you can continue to be annoyed or you can try turning on your own favorite music. Play it at a volume you're comfortable with so that you can sink into your music. Hopefully you will find the moment of disruption is quickly forgotten.

Music can change your mood regardless of whether you are a trained musician, a passive listener sitting at an intersection, a performer, an audience member, a Ruth, or a Warren.

Music can permeate your emotional essence—what some people call "heart" and others "soul"—in a way that written words cannot do alone. When we added melody to Kate's poetic words the emotion of the words came to life. Kate was able to experience her written words and feel it in a new way. And the best part about using music triggers intentionally to help make yourself happy, is that your perception of all that is around you changes for the better, and, that feeling is contagious. People recognize when someone is feeling happy and joyful, and that can make them feel happier and more joyful themselves.

Mark: Trigger the Good that Lies Beneath

Mark was very unhappy and didn't have a lot of energy most of the time. He knew about the power of music and thought he was doing all the right things with music. His doctor actually recommended that he find something he had previously enjoyed to help him feel better about life.

After some soul-searching, he remembered taking piano lessons as a child. His doctor encouraged him to return to his classical roots, believing that classical music would be best for him.

After pondering the idea, Mark bought himself a piano and once again took classical piano lessons as he did in his childhood. Mark started piano at the age of six, learned the saxophone as a teenager, and went on to jam in night clubs. He stopped playing when he married and had to do shift work.

Mark decided that he wanted to master the piano pieces he had learned as a boy. He bought recordings of the pieces he was learning and memorized how they sounded. He became quickly frustrated with his abilities and didn't feel he was anywhere close to how the recording sounded. That's when he called me.

During our first sessions together, the word "mastering" was brought up several times when he talked about what he was working on. He spoke with a sharp criticism towards music that was being created today. He complained that people were never taking music seriously enough, and were not learning it to perfection. Coming from my background with Mr. Nicholwitz, I experienced quite a different process with music, but I was intrigued with what Mark had to say. Mark said he loved music, but he was surprised when music didn't make him feel better. He noticed that every time he sat down to the piano he came away feeling more depressed and agitated with his family.

The man in front of me was someone who was full of anger. His stare was now vacant and the tone of his voice was clipped when he spoke. When we spoke about music, Mark was very clear that the music of his past was not nearly as refined as the music of today. The music he was working on now was written to perfection and it was up to him to match perfection.

When I asked whether pursuing those goals was working out for him he paused for a moment and said, "Not well."

I asked him to play the piece he had been practicing. It was flawless and void of any emotion. I told Mark that every note was perfect. I wanted to know what he thought was making it imperfect. He told me that what he was playing didn't sound like the recordings he had learned to appreciate. His anger dissipated when he told me that, but the tired eyes of a depressed person remained, so I knew that didn't help. But I had a suspicion about the real problem.

We discussed the actual performers, their processes, and their emotional states. We recognized that it would be next to impossible to ever recreate the recording since the performers were drawing on their emotions from their own experiences and transferring their heart and soul into the music. I suggested that we needed to step back from the mastery and think about music in a different way.

Mark agreed and he finally was able to realize that he needed to feel music again. That would not happen if perfection was his goal. Together, we decided we needed to help Mark find a new path, to interrupt his pattern of practicing classical music repeatedly to achieve perfection and to use music solely for self-expression.

We started the next session by talking about his favourite music from high school. He recalled that the band, Queen, recorded one his favourite albums, and he began to reminisce. It was the first time I saw him smile. Stories from his high school days immediately followed. He was a popular, outgoing youth who liked to socialize. When he listened to the song "Bicycle Race" by Queen, he was always with several friends in his parent's basement. They would recline on couches while some of the boys played shuffle board. Without any cues from me he said, "I haven't listened to that album for years."

I asked, "What do you feel would happen if you did."

He responded "Well, just thinking about the album brought a flood of memories back to me. I guess more of that and—a bit of fun." He smirked a little again.

Music was in Mark's life; however he had not yet chosen music for the purpose of making himself feel more able and active in his life. When his doctor recommended he do something he used to enjoy. Mark had forgotten that taking classical piano lessons as a child was the first time he experienced anxiety and pressure. Classical music was, in other words, a negative trigger for Mark because his focus was on reaching perfection with it. If that was his intention to begin with, then it would have been fine, but his intention was to change his mood and be more available to his family. On the other hand, the music he enjoyed during his high school days could take him back to a time when he felt less pressure and more freedom. That music was the positive trigger and that's what Mark needed to focus on.

All good strategies are best if used with the right intention—music is no different.

As Mark worked towards mastering those classical pieces, he was transported back to the unpleasant piano lessons from his childhood. By introducing a new music trigger based on positive past experiences Mark was able to move forward in meeting his goal of feeling better, more productive, and happier.

Music is often in the background—as we drive, as we clean the house, write a paper, or sing with the kids. But I hope you're really starting to understand what happens when we bring music into the foreground and use it with intention.

My work has shown me that by using music according to certain guidelines and with intent, it is possible to bring positive change to your daily life. The first step is to truly understand your triggers. These triggers are innately connected to your feelings and memories. When you gain a better understanding of your auditory triggers, it can help to add new music and sounds into your environment that trigger positive responses.

When to Hire a Music Therapist

Because triggers and anchors can be complicated, sometimes hiring a professional Music Therapist can be most helpful in sorting this out. Because it is a field that is not well understood, here are some pointers about us as professionals and music therapy in general.

Music therapy is an allied health profession and is used in healthcare facilities, education systems, corporations, and private residences/agencies. A Music Therapist undergoes rigorous training to use music intentionally to help clients reach individualized goals. They are specifically trained to distill the latest science in music and medicine into practical, therapeutic applications to use with clients of all ages.

Many people, young and old, are living with a wide array of physical and emotional needs: decline in motor functioning, social isolation, depression, anxiety, confusion, lack of focus, and physical pain. There is much evidence to indicate that music therapy can improve mood, mobility, memory and language. Music Therapist's also work with some of our most vulnerable including youth at risk, individuals with brain injury, those with mental health issues, learning challenges or dementia, and those in palliative care and long-term care. Professionals, educators and corporations access the services of Music Therapists to incorporate the health benefits of using music with intention at home and work. Ideally, every healthcare facility, employee assistance program and learning centre would have a certified Music Therapist available to work with every person who seeks change in their state of being.

There does seem to be confusion around using music for our own personal therapeutic benefit (such as discussed throughout this book) and those trained in the profession of music therapy.

A Music Therapist is foremost certified to be able to help individuals and is trained to ensure that music is used under the highest of ethical standards and with the largest body of knowledge. As we have identified throughout this book, music, a powerful resource, can do great things but can also cause harm by bringing up lost or undesired memories and emotions. It can strike tones that hurt your ears, or it can take individuals into a place of agitation. The Music Therapist monitors each individual response carefully and adjusts the treatment plan accordingly.

When selecting a Music Therapist look for someone who:

1. **Is certified** - Countries throughout the world have national certification programs for Music Therapists who have graduated with the prescribed educational requirements including supervised clinical work.

2. **Participates in on-going education** - A degree, and even a license, may not guarantee the effectiveness of a Music Therapist. It is important you ensure that they go beyond their certification. The therapist you consider should demonstrate their participation in ongoing education. This indicates that the therapist has initiative and a passion for their profession. It will also help you identify where their interests lie. Is their continuing education related to the goals you have for yourself?

3. **Has good rapport with you** - Even the most perfect, experienced therapist on paper may not be the right fit for you unless you can identify with them and their personality. Your

relationship with the therapist is essential to the process, so it is important to find someone with whom you feel connected and with whom you feel safe. The areas you work on will depend on whether you are hoping to be: challenged, validated, inspired, or transformed. A good therapist is going to take time to get to know you and what your goals are throughout your course of treatment.

Questions to help guide you to your desired Music Therapist include but are not limited to:

1. ***What expertise do you have in the area I am hoping to develop, change, or improve?*** Although the therapist doesn't necessarily need previous experience in helping with your exact problem, the therapist should be at least familiar with your type of situation and be prepared to tell you how they've helped others in similar circumstances.

2. ***What do they think is usually helpful for the needs you have described?*** This question will give you some idea as to the process the therapist will use and what has proven effective in the past.

3. ***What is their fee?*** In most cases you will be paying for a Music Therapist out of your agency budget or individual pocket, although there is increased support through private insurance and government funding. During the first meeting, you and the therapist will determine the approximate length of therapy necessary to help with your particular issues and goals. This should help determine a "ballpark" figure for the total cost of therapy. To investigate standard prices in your community you can visit: Professional Associations for Music Therapists:
Canada - www.musictherapy.ca
United States - www.musictherapy.com
World Federation - www.wfmt.info

A Music Therapist does two important things:

1. Sets the intention of the session based on the client's goals. Before entering a music therapy session a Music Therapist takes time to plan a suitable program aimed at specific goals.

2. Creates and continues to modify an ongoing program for the client. A music therapy session may have a general framework, but it is not something that is ever by rote. It is in a constant state of improv (musical flux)—moving from one feeling or experience to another—flowing seamlessly depending on where the client needs to go. The energy in the room is constantly monitored and the therapist uses the responses that happen in the moment to guide them to the next moment.

Science has finally caught up with what Music Therapist's have witnessed for many decades: that music can change the way a person feels, thinks and behaves.

Thanks also to fMRI machines and dedicated researchers, the general public has been awakened to the power behind using music in almost every health and educational context. All good strategies (and therapy) are best if used with the right intention—music is no different.

Music triggers, both positive and negative, surround us. What triggers one person's "happy," triggers another person's anguish. Classical music, for example, is thought of as the universal soother—that's obviously not always the case. Volume, something I've not talked a lot about yet, can also play a part. My publisher, whom you met in the forward, loves music but stopped listening to it for some odd reason. When she excitedly called me after reading this chapter on triggers and said, "it's the volume, silly," I had to smile. Her husband loves music too but he always plays it too loud for Patricia's taste. So listening to music in their car or in their house became an "either/ or" scenario. Either the music was on way too loud for Patricia's comfort or not on at all. Once she explained the idea of triggers to her husband, he was willing to compromise when they were together and music filled their home once again.

Because we are on the quest for wellness and betterment, our goal is to Trigger Our Happy as often as possible. In order to trigger our happy, it is important we first find the music that we can then use to help us get to where we want to go. Once you become aware of your triggers, you have the chance to use them proactively to your benefit. In some extreme cases it may be best to access your local Music Therapist to guide you through the process of identifying and finding new music triggers that can work towards your desired goals. Paying attention to what you like and don't like can be the start of not only understanding your triggers but living a life accompanied by the music and sounds that help you instead of harm you.

Exercise: Trigger Your Happy

1. Imagine a particularly stressful day. Imagine feeling over-whelmed and perhaps frustrated with the state of your home and the tasks and people in your work life. Perhaps you feel anxious around a particular person, or perhaps something has just happened that makes you uncomfortable and you know you will have to deal with it.

2. Imagine how your body physically feels when these stresses occur. What is your breathing pattern? Do you feel any particular pressure points in your body? Is there a weariness not there previously?

3. Once you have visualized this feeling, imagine you have just arrived home. You go to your favourite place where you can relax, begin to unwind from the day, and collect your thoughts. Suddenly, you remember a critical appointment was scheduled and you have only thirty minutes to get there on time! But your body is not ready to move.

4. What music would help you feel better immediately, help motivate you, and charge you enough so you don't feel so over-whelmed? The piece you choose should take you out of your current emotional state and move you into your more desired and needed emotional state.

5. Mentally go through your music library[14] and find just the right music. If it is difficult to find an actual song, then identify a particular singer or a certain genre of music. In your mind, play as much of this song as you can for the next thirty to sixty seconds then record how your physical and emotional state has changed.

6. Even if you didn't do the above activity, my hunch is that a song came to mind that allowed you to feel a shift. How quickly did that shift occur?

7. The application of music can swiftly decrease stress and can be life-changing. In many instances, the key to this transformation is personal music preference. In the visualization exercise music sparked the inner working systems that can jolt us into action. The piece selected may inspire you to some degree by affecting your mind and simultaneously causing physical changes. Regardless of the music genre you selected, it can take effect in a split second. One of the myths of music is that you need to select an up tempo piece in order to feel more motivated. The tempo of the piece is not as relevant as the emotional state the piece evokes in you.

8. Music that triggers Inspiration in you first is music that motivates you later.

9. When you start consciously using music to help you enhance your good emotions or change undesirable ones, the first thing to do is figure out what music you like when you're feeling up or when you're feeling blue. Get a notebook or sit down at your computer and go through this list:

10. What are your favourite songs right now?

11. What songs from your past, when you hear them give you a strong feeling? (concentrate on the songs that evoke good feelings)

12. What style of music do you listen to frequently?

13. Next to those songs and styles of music add a second column to identify the emotions that surface when you hear the music. Our goal in this case is to focus on our perceived good feelings, whatever those may be for you. If you bump into a few bruising songs along the way put those aside for now. The goal is to curb stress, boost morale and restore health.

CHAPTER 4

Find Your Music

"No two people on earth are alike, and it's
got to be that way in music, or it isn't music."
Billie Holiday

I hope by now you see how using music intentionally in our lives is very beneficial. Throughout the book I've been asking you, what if we could do more with music? What would happen if we made a small perspective shift and brought music more consciously into the foreground? What benefits could we anticipate in our mood, our level of stress, and our view on those around us?

While we have explored a few exercises to use music intentionally, we finally have arrived at my very favorite part: helping you find your music so you can reach your goals. In other words, you now get to fully discover your listening habits, your music preferences, and life's soundtrack so that you can use music with as much clarity and purpose as you can.

Our listening habits are the routines and behaviours we have that add to our auditory diet—i.e. when we turn on the radio or when we turn music on or off.

Part of my current listening habits is at my local coffee shop. Nothing makes me happier than great coffee, comfortable seats, plug-in availability for my laptop, and a great mix of music to inspire and spark my creativity while working on daily tasks. I can count on the music to enhance the bigger experience and would notice if it was absent.

Music preferences are music selections or styles that we naturally gravitate to either intellectually or emotionally. The reasons for the gravitation vary from person to person based on many factors including but not limited to mood, personal associations, and social pressures.

My music preferences are different depending on the month or even the time of day. Even if you have been taking a break from music and prefer silence more often than sound, that is still a preference. When you are in a positive mood, music can validate and even increase the emotion that you are feeling when you choose the right music. Knowing your music preferences will help you have your best triggers readily available so that you can snap yourself into the mood you want to be in.

I have already talked briefly about the idea of life's soundtrack. Your life's soundtrack is selecting the songs from your music library—all the music you have encountered throughout your lifetime—that represent key events and memories (both good and bad) in your life. When we work through the development of our life's soundtrack it gives us a glimpse into how our music choices over a long period of time affect us.

Our music soundtrack contains many music messengers. For example, Neil Young and Johnny Cash may speak to you with their way of writing and singing music in a way that almost forces you to want to get deeper into the men and the stories they have to share through their music. The way they speak to you then helps guide you through difficult times or experiences in your life. Specific songs or styles of music can eventually become your anchor songs, songs that anchor you to a feeling and when you hear that specific piece you feel rooted into that same emotional state time and time again.

Four Steps to Finding Your Music

Finding your music can be a joyous experience and it can also be quite complex. Many of us have layers of history with music, many associations, some even forgotten until you take the time to think about it. I have heard many a Music Therapist, after spending so much time with others and their music, say "I have lost my own." I have also heard professionals who are now working from ivory towers say "I forgot how deeply I love music, after being challenged to hear it again." Most recently I was asked by the National Association for the Hard of Hearing to speak to their group because, "we don't want our members giving up on music."

Although I have made the following steps simple I am not for one moment thinking that the internal processes you will go through to find the answers are anything like simple. Music is so deeply connected to your emotions and histories, and we all know how complex those can be at times. What I do encourage you to do is go through this part at your own speed. Don't rush. Give yourself the time to TUNE IN to your music. Let it help you navigate you through your values and help you get to where you want to go.

Together we will go back through your life and rediscover what music made you feel good and brought you joy. We will pay attention to how you use music right now so that you can be more aware of how to use if effectively in the future. And best of all, you will make a playlist of songs that will help you in various situations in life so that you can go through your day calmer, happier, and even maybe more in control.

As the introduction to part four hints at, there are four steps you need to take to find your music. They are:

1. Document Your Life's Soundtrack
2. Determine Your Current Music Listening Habits
3. Identify Your Music Preferences
4. Establish Your Anchor Songs

You can either read through this section quickly and get a sense as to where we are going with finding your music or you can work through the activities slowly, in a group, or with a friend. Regardless of how you do it, let the music that comes up become a part of you even from the moment you feel it. It is in the feeling of the music and allowing it to affect your emotional state that you will gain the most benefit of finding the music that matters most to you.

Step One: Document Your Life's Soundtrack

We are always collecting music. Some of our collection gets released over time and temporarily forgotten while other music memories endure throughout our lifetime. However, under the right circumstances all music is retrievable meaning that it's something that we can remember when the conditions are right.[1] What you may find most interesting about this exercise though, is that by taking time to look at our music history, we can step back from our lives and take time to look at ourselves in a more objective way, which can be very therapeutic.

Everyone has a unique life soundtrack that highlights the bumps, joys, and bruises of life. Our lives can be documented with music. Movies, television, live experiences and passive listening all contribute to our life soundtrack. I have read magazines that suggest we don't add much new music after the age of thirty.[2] Perhaps that is why we all end up listening to the oldies station at some point in our life. I have also noticed, however, (and if my children are any example), that many children listen to the same music we once did. I mean exactly the same. The same artist. The same song. I have heard some people say something like, "See your generation can't even come up with any of your own music because ours was so superior." Now I am not naming names but I know many who have thought the same thing.

My life's soundtrack is now meshed with my husband, my friends and my children. My son is a wonderful saxophone player and dreams of being a jazz or blues musician. His music preferences go further back than my generation as he loves the sounds and swings of Charlie Parker and the arrangements of Miles Davis. My daughter has become an East Coast Fiddler and plays in a local group. When she plays the toe stomping Rigs and Reels she captures the attention of many seniors who hear this style of music and stand up and swing the person next to them. Getting to know yourself and others through music that has been a part of your life is a wonderful exercise and develops tolerance for generational differences and historical differences. Because of their music preferences, I have broadened my life's soundtrack.

Take time to access your music history. Try to document your songs chronologically. Memories are most likely attached to your music. As you go through this exercise, remember to make a note about those memories in the side column.

Our earliest music memories are some of the most long lasting memories we may have. Pay particular attention to these and the feelings that are evoked when you think of them. I remember the first time I heard "One Tin Soldier." To this day, I recall every word as if I had just learned it yesterday. It conjures up feelings of togetherness, and I obviously still love it.

To document your life's soundtrack is simple but does take time. You are going through your entire life, from birth to now. The following chart illustrates how you're going to proceed through this exercise.

Exercise: Your Personal Soundtrack

With a piece of paper by your side or on your computer, construct the following chart. If you can do this on the computer, that would be best because you're obviously going to need more space than what's given here to write down all the music you listened to at whatever age and the memories associated with that music. If you don't use a computer, that's fine. Just make one age category per page. That way, if you need to use more paper—say for your teen years - you can do that and not get the age groups mixed up (that's very important actually. You want to recognize when you were listening to what music).

Worksheet: Personal Soundtrack

Age	The Music You Listened To During this Time	Associated Memories
Birth to Grade School		
Grade School		
Adolescence		
Adulthood		
Later Life		

All worksheets are also downloadable at www.tuneintomusic.ca

From Birth to Grade School (Earliest Memories)

The first category is the music from your early years. Some of you may remember a lot of the music and other sounds you were exposed to at this time. Some of you may remember very little. Don't worry about the quantity. It's what you do remember that's important. You may use some of those old songs to help soothe you—like maybe remembering the lullaby your mother sang to you when you were a baby.

If you have young children in your life, I want to pause for a moment and review a few important details. From as early as in our mother's womb there is evidence that babies are aware of and respond to music and different sounds.[3] Moments after birth, a baby may turn in the direction of a voice or sound in search of its source. Newborns quickly learn to differentiate their mother's voice from others. There is a great deal of evidence around the connection between stimuli received in early childhood and brain growth; therefore, exposing children to music early on can have overall significance for a child's well-being.[4]

There seems to be a lot of information pertaining to the benefits of music during brain development including improved memory and learning. However, what I find most interesting is how music attracts our attention at an early age. My children were very young when Barney first came on the scene. Reluctantly the program became a staple in our home due to the fact that my children were completely transfixed and immobile for the duration of the show, giving me time to complete other tasks. There was never any doubt that the people from the Barney show had fully researched what captivates children. My two children who were always actively wrestling, yelling, laughing, and pushing toys would stop everything and just stare and occasionally point at the big purple dinosaur.

I decided it was time for some research of my own. During the next few episodes of Barney, I found myself sitting on the floor next to my children while using a stopwatch. My hypothesis: the Barney people had perfected a child's timing for maintaining attention. I wanted to learn what that timing was. I wanted to assess the music triggers, how often they happened, and how much time lapsed in between. My living room trial showed that the music in Barney was regular, repeatable, and predictable. That made me think of about my own early years of television programming with Mr. Dressup, Mr. Rogers, and Sesame Street. I could see a similar pattern. We always knew when a song was about to happen, and even though we had heard it many times before, we loved it even more. As I watched Barney, I found myself bouncing my head a little and smiling as my children sang along.

By taking the time to explore the benefits that music can offer your children, you'll be uncovering something priceless: your child's imagination and inner sense of creativity and self-expression. Children seem to absorb music through their entire bodies, as indicated by the spontaneous humming and movement I have witnessed. They seem to appreciate predictable and repetitive music that can be easily assimilated and familiarized. There are moments when a song strikes such a strong chord that a person retains the song for many hours, days, weeks, or even months. Just ask any parent from the 1990's who was trapped with Barney's "I Love You" on a long car ride home.

However, it shouldn't be assumed that children do not appreciate a wide variety of music. I am sure you know a child who loves rock and roll, classical, jazz, reggae, or country music. There is enough evidence to say that our music preferences start forming before the age of two.[5] Being exposed to such a large amount of music could also open the doors to future experiences otherwise unavailable. Who knows, they may become very passionate about a certain type of music, or want to play an instrument or simply just want to sing because it makes them feel good.

I personally have very few music memories prior to school, but I re-member many sounds. I grew up in a seventies suburban town, where homes were moved from acreages to quiet streets. The familiar sights and sounds of the time were typically mothers hollering for their children who were nine houses away, children riding their bikes in the middle of the road, lawn mow-ers sputtering and rumbling along as they attacked each blade of grass, dogs barking and howling at other dogs as they walked in their territory, and the occasional radio blasting from a new Camero or Firebird. These sounds are as vivid to me now as they were when I experienced them for the first time. This was my neighborhood music, and I love it when I hear those same sounds now, wherever I am. It makes me feel warm and loved, just as I did when I was a kid.

Grade School

Grade school is a time when group music is introduced to many children, and we may or may not be listening to the radio or songs on T.V. shows. What is most interesting to me about this stage in our lives is how we process music. The brain undergoes rapid neural development during the first years of life and new neural networks are formed more rapidly than at any other time.[6] Even though grade school is when many of us experience our first formal music training in choir, band, or private lessons in mid-childhood, these pathways are already being primed. We don't keep what we don't need, or, more accurately, we don't keep what we don't use.

I experienced my first "live" music in grade two. Half a school year had passed before Mr. Trudea walked into our class with a guitar case in hand. I had never seen someone make music before with just their voice and a guitar. Mr. Trudea sat on a chair and faced the entire class. We were all huddled together on the carpet looking straight up at him expectantly. He began to strum and sing with a clear voice, allowing us to absorb every word. I was in awe. His guitar had a worn patch under his strumming hand and he smiled as he sang.

We learned many new songs that we had never heard before. Goodbye Fred Rogers. I will miss you Friendly Giant. Move over Mr. Dressup and welcome in Mr. Bob Dylan, Original Caste and Friendly John Denver. Repeatedly, we sang "Blowing in the Wind," "One Tin Soldier" and "Country Roads." Music was no longer stuck in a radio. My music tastes continued to form and became very personal during these childhood years.

The brain goes through many processes in helping us interpret the music that we hear. Our ears become attuned to certain styles and textures which are specifically intriguing to us.[7] That's what I want you to explore in this age category—those styles and textures that you gravitated towards in the music you remember. These can be accessed again and used as positive triggers.

Adolescence

It is during our teen years that music seems to be associated with a lot of firsts: first dance, first kiss, first love, first break up. Perhaps that is why the music of our teen years seems to linger far into adulthood if not forever.

Teens have a very personal and self-centred relationship with music. They personalize the songs and validate their angst with the lyrics and melodies they internalize. And it's the music of our teen years that we often revisit when we need a boost or we want to feel carefree when life's load is getting to be too heavy.

When I was a teen I was no athlete but several of my friends were. Carolyn was the most talented, natural athlete in school. Her long legs and long hair would just float along the earth and no one could keep up to her, especially me. That did not deter me from wanting to be a close friend of hers. At recess she would teach me wonderful tricks that I could do on the monkey bars including walking across the top and practicing triple axel-ish movements off the side of the posts.

I was on my third try to get the flip just right when I landed on the ground and heard a terrible crack. I saw my ankle pointing awkwardly. My mind went blank as a teacher came and carried me into the school. Mom picked me up and took me to the doctor. Timing could not have been worse. It was Halloween and my costume was waiting at home. This was the first year that I was going trick or treating with a large group of fun friends without parent supervision.

The doctors were able to set the ankle with a cast, but it didn't help my spirits and the profound disappointment I was experiencing. The only thing that could turn this event around was something bigger than going out with my friends on Halloween and more distracting than my broken ankle. The answer came in the form of a surprise gift.

As I lay in bed at home, dejected, Mom reached into a plastic bag and pulled out a thin cardboard package. I sat up and unwrapped the album. Speechless, I saw the face on the front of the album. Staring at me was my heart throb—Shaun Cassidy. With his blue eyes and blond wavy hair, I could feel Shaun looking right through me. I forgot about what I was missing that evening. It took me a full hour to carefully unwrap and play the entire album while flipping through the inner pages of quotes, photos and song lyrics. I was completely absorbed.

Whenever I have my music therapy participants begin to explore their music choices from their teen years the music triggers are fast and furious. It seems that these music memories are some of the most strongly anchored memories that can take us back to an array of emotions and situations of the time. When I think back to all the music of my teen years, I remember lying on my girlfriend's bed, listening to ABBA and the Bee Gees. It was a feeling of belonging and acceptance. Music filled me up, and whenever I hear those songs, I get those same feelings.

Adulthood

As we enter in adulthood we leave behind many of the social pressures that can go along with listening to music during our youth. It is easy to get caught up in the relationships behind the music without taking time to actually choose the music you want to listen to. As adults, preferences become more settled with your favourite radio stations and albums. However what continues is the establishment of music associations with personal encounters, and it is very important to record those on your chart as well.

New Husband: What the Funk?

The first time I saw my future husband across a crowded dance floor, he was three inches taller than anyone else. With his head bobbing up and down to the music, his eyes were closed, and he had a huge smile on his face. I can remember watching him for a couple of dances thinking what an incredibly happy, fun person he must be. Little did I know that he was really serious, not too funny, and a computer geek.

The music exposed what we now call his "inner James." First impressions matter and what I saw was someone who came to life when music played—especially Funk music. This is also known as Disco, however "inner James" assures me it is Funk and that they are totally different. At one point in the evening he walked over and asked me to dance. I thought my heart was going to fall out of my chest. The music started, we faced each other and danced. James closed his eyes tight, flung his head back and moved like a crazy man on the floor. He was in perfect time and not a bad dancer. He looked great but I don't think he really knew how I looked as he rarely looked at me.

He must have enjoyed my spiritual energy as he called me a week later and proposed six weeks after that. Now, twenty years later, James still gets on any dance floor, flings his head back, closes his eyes, sinks right into the music and the Funk gods take him away.

After my husband and I were married a few weeks, we began to settle into our personal routines—the routines that re-enter your life after the initial "We must be together at all times, fully embraced in love."

One of my favourite rituals is taking a bath, using an exorbitant amount of night cream, getting into bed, and reading eight or nine pages of my book in silence. I also quickly learned about my new husband's bedtime routines. He liked to do a few sit-ups and push-ups, get into bed and then turn the music on! At first I thought it was a phase, but then I learned that music was relaxing to him and he played it before bed, every night, since he was a child. Somehow I missed this on my pre-marriage questionnaire.

He said music soothed him. It removed the day's stress. For me, music sparks my creativity and imagination and engages my brain. That's the last thing I wanted before bed. Silence was what I desired so my brain would slow and ease into a deep sleep. So with my night-creamed face, I sat and stared straight at the ceiling hearing music. How was I ever going to sleep again?

Being a new wife I didn't think it appropriate for me to tell him how much I hated it especially since I used music every day. It somehow seemed inconsistent, but I wasn't sure what my options were. We eventually discussed it and found an easy solution—earphones. He understood my dilemma although I think he still questions how a Music Therapist can be so negatively affected by music. To this day he puts in his earphones, turns on his favorite selections, and falls asleep.

A life-time relationship with my husband has meant a blending of many things. It meant joining two very different pasts into one place and then growing new memories together. Our music has been no exception. We both came from a "music is incredibly important to me" background.

I have learned a lot about my husband through his music. He has introduced or re-introduced me to individuals and groups that I did not have a strong connection to in the past including Elton John, Tower of Power and all things Funk. I in turn introduced him to Lena Horn, Willie Nelson, YES and George Michael (post-Wham). We also got together on some pretty significant music in both our lives – James Taylor, Aretha Franklin, and Luther Vandross. Together, we have explored music at festivals and listened to what our friends share with us. Later on, our children began to contribute to our never-ending soundtrack (Taylor Swift, Pink, Bruno Mars). We have thousands of songs of blended music that represent us as individuals and as a family. Our personal and family soundtrack continues to expand and represent where we have come from and who we are today, and I am very grateful that I knew from the beginning of my relationship with James to keep track of the songs, the sounds, and the memories so that we could call upon them again when we needed or wanted to.

Later Life

For many of the seniors I have worked with music played a significant role in their lives. I cannot count the number of stories I have heard about their live music experiences including singing around the piano at many social functions. I had the opportunity of going back in time by singing in a trio that specialized in music from the thirties, forties, and fifties. We were invited to sing at many dance halls and legions and I was always amazed at the dancing skills of the audience members. It seems that many of the seniors I work with in our community know a lot of the same music including many of the lyrics. Music can capture an entire time and can help you celebrate the life you have lived.

Gwen: Will you Remember Me?

Being aware of your soundtrack can have some profound consequences. For Gwen, music enabled her to become all that she could be just a month before she would die. Gwen, a fifty-five-year old blonde beauty, sat in a warmly decorated room near the window. Sixteen months prior, she was diagnosed with cancer. Now she sat in a hospice room near the outskirts of town. She was a model patient going through many rounds of chemotherapy and radiation. After her initial diagnosis and for several months, her family and friends were not aware of her cancer. Gwen would rarely ask for help. The care staff were just around the corner and would often enter her room to check on her. Except for occasional pain medicine she would smile at them and say, "I'm okay.' Her husband had passed away many years before and she would often say she was glad he went first as this would have been very difficult for him.

She never expected the breast cancer to metastasize at such a rapid rate until she heard those fateful words, "There is nothing more we can do for you but give you a comfortable place to rest." She had dreaded telling her only daughter and her sister the news. When she told them, they both broke down in tears and were soon making sure the doctors had done everything they could. Now in hospice, Gwen did all she could in her fragile state to prepare her loved ones for the inevitable.

When I was introduced to Gwen, she was wearing a colorful head scarf that covered what was once blond hair. Pictures of her and her family were all around the room, interspersed with colorful paintings and drawings.

"Come, sit close to me, I have been expecting you," she said.

She pointed to the chair next to her chair by the window and rested her hand on my shoulder as I sat down. She turned slightly and in a sweet, gentle voice said, "I have had a lot of time to process what is happening to me, and understand I must die. I am worried about my daughter, Hailey, and my sister Julia. They are very angry. She took a deep breath and said, "They are not accepting that this is happening to me or to them." She brushed a few strands of what was left of her hair away from her eyes and said, "I need you to help me."

She pointed to several pieces of art around the room that she had created over her lifetime. She spoke of how her daughter was as passionate about painting as she was. "It's in the genes," she assured me and mentioned to me her sister had started taking lessons over the past few years. She told me that she had some ideas of how to integrate art and music while also helping her daughter and sister come to the understanding that she is going to die— and soon.

Just as my grandmother had a plan years earlier reaching into a desk drawer for my grandfather's favorite song, Gwen's plan also rested in the desk drawer she had asked me to open. "Take out the small stack of papers." I looked at the ten songs in front of me.

"Will you please play the songs on your guitar on Saturday and meet us here precisely at 2:00 p.m.?"

Before I had the chance to say, "I don't work weekends," her blue eyes crinkled and she touched my shoulder again. I would change my weekend plans.

That Saturday, I had the songs prepared and arrived precisely at 2:00 p.m. Her daughter and sister were sitting on either side of her. She asked me to sit in the corner on a chair. Once we were all in place she sat up a little further in her bed. She started by saying, "Thank you for coming." She then turned to her daughter Hailey and her sister Julia and said, "I invited you here today because we need to say goodbye." Silence. "I know that this is hard for you as it is for me, so I came up with an idea that could perhaps help all of us. Hailey will you please go into the side closet and take out the piece of canvas I asked Julia to bring last week."

Hailey slowly walked over to the closet, opened the door, and brought the canvas that had been leaning against the wall inside. "Julia will you please reach into that top drawer and bring out the pastels that one of the nurses brought for me." Julia walked to the end of the bed and opened the top drawer where the pastels were. There were many colors.

Once the two women were back on either side of Gwen, they heard her speak again. "I have asked Jennifer to play ten songs today. During the first song I am going to start drawing and when the song ends I am going to pass the canvas to you Julia and you are going to continue the picture adding in whatever the music brings to your mind.

"When the second song is finished then you will pass the canvas to Hailey who is going to continue from where you left off. We will pass the canvas back and forth after every song for the first nine songs and then relax and reflect during song number ten. The tenth song is a special song I have selected for the three of us."

Julia and Hailey stared at Gwen not saying a word. Gwen's determination was clearly visible on her face and to say anything would break the spell she had on all of us. Hailey passed the canvas to Gwen and reached into the box on Julia's lap to select a couple of pastels. I took a deep breath. When Gwen looked at me and nodded slightly I started to play. I could not see what was being created on the canvas, but I could definitely see a transformation happening on the faces of the three women. The canvas did what it was supposed to—passing between each family member at the end of each song. No tears were shed, just a change of focus and an occasional smile as they passed on their contribution.

We sang many powerful songs. Lean On Me. You've Got a Friend. True Colors. Soon it was time for the last song. I was nervous as I strummed the first few chords as I knew there would be no more pastels on the canvas, only reflections of what was created. The highly emotionally charged song Gwen selected as the last piece was Louis Armstrong's, "What a Wonderful World."

I see trees of green, red roses too
I see them bloom for me and you
And I think to myself what a wonderful world.

I see skies of blue and clouds of white
The bright blessed the day, the dark sacred night
And I think to myself what a wonderful world.

The colors of the rainbow so pretty in the sky
Are also on the faces of people going by
I see friends shaking hands saying how do you do
But they're really saying is I love you.

I hear baby's crying and I watched them grow
They'll learn much more than I'll ever know
And I think to myself what a wonderful world.
Yes, I think to myself what a wonderful world.

Gwen put a few finishing strokes on the canvas and then held it up for each of them to look at. The tears they held back released and two arms went behind Gwen in an embrace as they gazed at the piece of art they created. I finished the last words and put my guitar down quietly. Gwen passed the canvas in my direction as both her daughter and sister's faces were now embedded in both of her shoulders. I carefully put the canvas on a high shelf looking down on them so it could dry. It was a beautiful meadow with flowers of many colours. I left the room so the women could say goodbye.

Gwen had set the intention of using her life's music soundtrack as the backdrop to an already powerful relationship. It was a non-verbal means of sharing herself and her heart, and those songs allowed her to say a touching goodbye.

Step Two: Determine your Listening Habits

While writing this book, I spent a substantial amount of time addressing the music in my own life. I was surprised how little I was using music outside of my work. Once I started researching and watching YouTube more regularly, I found a way to access and enjoy new music for the first time since my twenties. Reading articles and books about what music is doing for people reminded me about the uniqueness of my music preferences and experiences.

Our music listening habits are unique to each one of us. Fortunately, music is also accessible to most of us and we don't need a high dosage to make a significant impact. Although the quantity of music I listen to is less than when I was younger, I have noticed that my perceived impact quotient has gone up. When I listen to live or recorded music, I am more often completely engrossed in the experience and I continue to add new music to my collection.

Some of my music listening habits include:
- Hearing a song I like and adding it to my current playlist.
- Watching Facebook posts to identify my friends favourite music and clicking to either remind myself of the song or learn something new.
- Trying to learn all the words of a new song in my car (and old songs that I continue to mix up the lyrics to).
- Asking my children to play me some of the songs they like (often putting their radio station on for car rides).
- Starting with one Youtube video and then seeing what other

Youtube videos are suggested (I rekindled my love of many of the artists from my past this way.)

- Taking time to day dream at a coffee shop when a great song comes over the speaker system and if I don't know the song I hold up an app that tells me what it is and I can add it to my playlist.
- Talking about music memories with my friends.

The simplest way I know of to help you figure out what your current music listening habits are is to go through the following questions. I developed it several years ago when I didn't have access to a tool to help my clients identify their listening habits even though I knew how important it was to

Worksheet: Current Listening Habits

Question	Tuned In Answer If this were to mean something, what could it mean?
Where have you listened to music over this past month?	
When do you not listen to music?	
How do you feel when you are not listening to music?	
How are you using music therapeutically in your life right now?	
If you are not using music - why do you think that is?	
If music no longer existed where would you miss it the most?	
How often in a day are you actively paying attention to music?	
Is music continually playing in your home or office?	

All worksheets are also downloadable at www.tuneintomusic.ca

do so. Have fun with the exercise. It's a great activity to work through with people at work, good friends or family members.

Pay particular attention to whether you see any patterns in your responses. As you identify those patterns, think about how you can use them—or change them—to help you develop a more intentional approach to music.

Step Three: Identify Your Preferences

Listening to a favorite song triggers a common pattern of brain activity, regardless of genre. That may explain why different people describe similar emotional feelings and memory responses when listening to their favorite piece of music, whether it is Bach or Eminem.

When one listens to preferred music, people often report the same response — experiencing personal thoughts and memories. Favourite songs bring about increased connectivity in a brain circuit associated with internally focused thoughts.

We are all aware to greater or lesser degree of what we like and don't like in music. Step 3 to finding your music is all about becoming aware of the three areas that make up your music preference: style preferences, tempo preferences, and tone preferences. Together they will give you your full-bodied list for music preferences.

Your preferences are your greatest triggers to snap you into the mood you want to be in. Our music soundtrack gives us a glimpse into how we are affected by our music choices over a long period of time. Marketing research has really taken this to heart. Companies spend time learning what would be the best music (or no music) to play in their retail outlet and advertisements. One woman said, "I hate when I walk into a retail store that is playing music I don't like."

I responded with, "Perhaps you are not the demographic they are marketing to."

She said she had never thought about that before.

There is a long-held theory that there is part of our mind that can recognize patterns within complex data but that we are hardwired to find simple patterns pleasurable.[8] This does not imply that human beings are simple, but it does seem to suggest that the mind likes to make sense of what it hears. Our minds feed on what they can easily understand and interpret. So whether you are a die-hard classicist or a pop diva it seems you choose the music you prefer by how you feel when you hear it.

Laura: Operatic Lullaby

Finding Laura's music preferences took time, but when we did, this little person who could barely communicate found a way to connect. During her birth, Laura's oxygen was deprived for twenty minutes requiring immediate resuscitation. She had no brainwave activity on two EEG tests and little hope she would survive, except in her parents' heart. When Laura's mother finally saw her baby, Laura required breathing assistance with a respirator. To connect to her daughter, her mom Lisa began to sing "Where Did You Go My Lovely"—a song she remembered from her own childhood. She arranged to have lullabies play continually near Laura's bed. Soon Laura began to breathe on her own.

When Laura turned four she plucked my guitar. It was the first time her parents witnessed her using her hands independently and unsupported. Soon Laura began to use her hands consistently. Other professionals insisted that Laura would have to "use her head" to push a switch or "eye gaze" to make choices. Today she uses her hands for both tasks. Laura reaches to strum the guitar with both hands and will alternate one hand then the other slowly and with intention.

As Laura grew with music, many non-music goals were achieved. However Laura, like many, became passionate about the music itself— for music's sake. When singing, Laura used her voice to produce long, dramatic tones, moving her lips to manipulate her voice very much like that of an opera singer. I suggested to Laura's family that opera music be played in the home. Laura's response to opera was evident the moment it first played. She began to cry and smile at the same time. Her parents claim it is the "style of music that makes her feel the most alive."

Each of us has a song or a special genre of music that taps into our core. As soon as we hear it, it is almost indescribable. It warms us. It makes us feel at home. Our music preferences do matter. I believe our preferences reflect who we are and that our preferences of how, why and what we listen to can be altered over our lifetime. Our differences in our preferences contribute to what makes us interesting, and identifying the various elements of those preferences definitely puts us in the driver's seat of using music intentionally.

Style Preferences

Style preferences are often one of the easiest markers of music preferences. This is the kind of music we like. From classical to country, there are definite styles that we gravitate towards. It is fun as well as important to recognize what your style preference are, but always leave yourself open to surprises. As your ability to use music intentionally gets better, you might find that one type of music style you didn't care for is now something you like.

Making people think about and experience music differently is what my work as a Music Therapist is all about. Here is one activity I use to help my clients begin thinking about their style preferences. Imagine that starting tomorrow you can only listen to one quadrant of music for the rest of your life. You can choose only one. Decide whether you are an A,B, C or D. As someone who listens to a wide array of music I know how difficult this is but just stick with me for a moment.

I need you to commit to your choice and allow yourself the feeling that comes from just having the one choice.

In my workshops I ask all the A's to stand. Then I introduce the A's as the most intelligent people in the room—these are the chess players, the academics, the ones that know stuff. The rest of the group, now unsure of this activity, give them a soft applause. I assure everyone that there are no wrong answers, but at this point no one believes me. The A's sit down and I ask the B's to stand next.

I introduce the B's as the most cheerful, reliable people in the room. Employers should hire them and their co-workers should invite them to their next social.

Next I ask the C's to stand. They comply but stand looking around the room a little to see how many of them there are. There tend to be fewer

C's than B's in the North American rooms I have visited. This is the time I joke that "those standing before you now may silently be thinking about how stupid this activity is." I inform the C's that they are curious, risk takers, and ask terrific questions; however they can often be disappointed with the answers.

Finally the D's. Those who have selected dance, hip hop and pop. Surprisingly enough, the group that stands before me is not necessarily all twenty-two-year olds. I have had rooms where people in their seventies will stand during this quadrant. Their rationale is, "I have always liked the popular music of the day, whatever it changes into." These people seem filled with confidence. They are energetic and full of fun. Once they are standing I let them know that I have some bad news for them. "D's have yet to be diagnosed." The room typically laughs as I lead into a discussion of how everyone felt about being stereotyped within a certain style of music.

I ask the group, "Is this music-based science?"

The answer is, "absolutely not." But what it does do is begin the conversation into the music we do listen to and what it potentially says about us—if anything at all. Perhaps it does speak to the lens through which we view the world. Perhaps there is enough truth in this one activity to get us questioning each other and identifying our differences. Perhaps music doesn't always bring us together under one room and actually highlights our greatest distinctions. If everyone liked the same music, would music carry the same amount of potency? The point is that what we are listening to right now, at this time in our life, has importance. It represents something: our current viewpoint, how we feel, where we are. But viewpoints and feeling change, and it is vital to allow your music preferences to change with those.

Tempo Preferences

Tempo is simply the pace of the music. Fast, slow, and every tempo in-between—music has them all. One of the most important elements of music that you can identify is what tempo resonates with you best. The following example isn't about music, but it is about sound and how viscerally we can react when that sound doesn't match the emotional or intellectual space we're in at the moment.

Victoria is a competent, clever, thoughtful, and skilled professional; however, when she communicates with people they are easily disinterested in what she has to say. When she finishes speaking a sentence, her listener's comment is often, "Good seeing you, I have to run."

When I noticed how Victoria was turning people away during her conversations I realized she speaks very slowly and adds in a lot of pauses while thinking before her next sentence. In addition, she has a very monotone voice. When she speaks, her listeners tended to speak more quickly and would fidget and look around while Victoria completes her thoughtful sentence. If you printed Victoria's thoughts, they would be articulate and meaningful. Unfortunately, because of her speed and lack of inflection she is unable to hold the listener's attention long enough to keep them engaged and interested in her conversation.

If we are truly music beings, and our walk, our talk, our voice, our manners can all be interpreted musically, then it is quite easy to start looking at ourselves through a music lens.

Everyone has a different tempo which affects those around us. My husband, James, begins to rev up at 8:30 p.m. This is when he is his most creative, expressive, and alert. I, on the other hand, love my evening rituals and looking forward to a wonderfully peaceful sleep. James often tries to engage me in enlightening conversation right before bed, and I inevitably disappoint him greatly with my nods of "yes, that sounds nice."

On the other hand, I wake up in the morning ready to go. I feel alive with endless enthusiasm. After much searching, I finally found where the "it's a beautiful day in the neighborhood this fine early morning" people are hiding —at the dog park. Happily, twice a week, I go to the mile-long park with other morning pet owners. We congregate and discuss how our dogs are communicating. With coffees in hand, the morning enthusiasts are up for an invigorating morning stroll in the dog park.

My upbeat and bright morning enthusiasm matches my morning music. I even keep the radio tuned in to my daughter's station of the night before so that when I wake up, I have energetic music to listen to.

The speed and manner in which we move, speak, laugh, complete tasks and present to others supports their perceptions of who we are. During a team-building workshop including Victoria, I had each of the group identify their daily tempo. I had purposefully paired Victoria with a fast speaker. I had each of the groups identify their daily tempos and the speed of activities such as going through email, answering questions, and verbally communicating with one another. I then placed them into separate groups—one fast and one slow person, as defined by themselves.

When I asked the group to identify who was the fast speaker between the two of them and who was the slow speaker, I immediately heard Victoria and her partner laugh. We then discussed what others perceive if the individual pace is too fast or too slow what it actually means when you speak at a specific speed. Responses included: "When I speak fast it means I am efficient."

Partners countered, "When you speak fast I am not certain you heard everything you needed to hear to complete the task correctly—it makes me nervous."

For the slow talkers, they said, "When I speak slowly it is because I am thinking carefully about what I am saying as I want to be accurate.

Their partners then said, "When you speak too slowly I get bored and feel like you are holding me up." While this is not a book on communication, the tempo of the music we choose to listen to is as important as timbre and volume.

Music is a many layered entity, and to use it the most effectively, it is important to note which music is important to you at various times in the day or for various moods. And it's not always a one-to-one correlation. Sometimes, when you're blue, you may find that faster tempo music is more helpful than slower music. And as always, there are no right or wrong answers. Rather it's all about paying attention to your relationship to music and what you need in that moment to help you.

Worksheet: Tempo Preferences

Question	Tuned In Answer If this were to mean something, what could it mean?
What speed of music do you prefer to wake up to?	
What speed of music do you prefer to go to sleep to?	
What speed of music would help you feel refreshed after a long day at work?	
What speed of music do you prefer to exercise to?	
What speed of music motivates you during a low time?	

All worksheets are also downloadable at www.tuneintomusic.ca

Mom: and the Chicken Dance

For my mom, the music she listened to post-divorce said a lot about what she was becoming or re-becoming. All parents embarrass their children.

My mom found that the best way to do this was to turn up the radio and dance in the kitchen. I remember one time when my mom heard a song she liked and started to do what I termed "the chicken" dance. She informed me later that it was actually called "the jive." Although I mocked her as she moved forward and backward, all the time her arms flying around her, I had to admit it was good to see her happy again. Mom and Dad had divorced a few years earlier and my Dad eventually remarried. Mom felt betrayed and alone. I don't remember her speaking ill of my dad, but I did notice she lost the spark that she once had. She became very thin and withdrawn while working three jobs. Seeing her reclaim the habit of letting loose and dancing to upbeat tempo music reminded me how she used to be—fun, happy, and free.

Timbre (Tone) Preferences

Different tones from different instruments will attract individuals in different ways just as different volumes of music will affect people. The same melody on the guitar will be responded to differently when played on a flute, violin, or voice. My job as a Music Therapist is to seek out the best combination of tones (the notes) and timbre (the sound of the instrument) that will motivate the individual.

Tones affect us everywhere. Some of these tones can annoy us to complete frustration; other tones can soothe us into dream land. At work, we have scores of tones around us and many of which we have absolutely no control over. Sometimes we may be even able to change these negative tones and in turn boost the spirits of the workplace.

Marie: and the Squeaky Chair

Exiting the elevator, I heard two loud voices at the nursing station heatedly discussing why a patient was not out of bed yet. The older of the two nurses with the name badge MARIE sitting in a wheeled chair pushed across the nursing station, grabbed some paper, slammed the cupboard door, and pushed her feet against the floor moving her chair back to the other side of the station. The chair had a terrible high- pitched squeak that followed her across desk area. I walked up to the desk and announced my arrival.

"I am here to speak to the nursing team about music therapy." Marie rolled her eyes.

"You're down the hall and to the right," she said, giving a short wave in that direction.

I walked slowly past many seniors in wheelchairs and beds. Their heads were down and many eyes were closed. Loud voices at the nursing station could still be heard.

I turned into the last room on the right where I was to speak to the nurses during shift change. I was told that I had precisely twenty minutes and running over time was not permitted. The table in front of me had sixteen chairs chaotically arranged around it. The table was full of papers and candy wrappers.

On the table, I placed a three-foot long aboriginal flute which I had purchased at a conference. The flute is a staple in my music kit. It is made from a single piece of cedar with a carving of an eagle on top. The creative artist who made it was both carpenter and a musician from a reserve in the state of Colorado. The tone was deep and mellow. One person commented, "it sounded like freedom, a place I want to go." For my newly gathered group of frustrated nurses, I hoped it would do the trick.

I waited for them at the front of the room. At precisely 3:00 p.m., the nurses entered the staff room with their baby blue and pink Tupperware containers of snacks and sat down.

I started with a few stats of what music can do for seniors—it could spark long forgotten memories, offer a sense of familiarity to those lost in dementia, and help them feel less isolated. Half the room seemed interested, but I noticed Marie was digging deep into her tupperware to find the last piece of chicken.

It was then looking straight at Marie, I said, "Music can help you too."

I continued, "When I came into the building I noticed that this is a very busy place. I imagine it can get quite stressful. Music in very short doses can make a big impact on your environment. Let me give you a small example." I reached behind me for my flute and put it up to my lips.

Marie was just about finished chewing her last piece of chicken when she said, "Well I hate music." No-one looked shocked or surprised by that comment.

I pulled the flute away from my mouth and said, "You are not alone. I have met others who have verbalized they do not like music. Sometimes music is just more noise that adds to the chaos and it is really silence we are seeking to help us de-stress." She nodded slightly.

"I am not expecting that everyone in this room will enjoy this instrument; however, because I can tell that you are a group that is sensitive to the sounds around you, I know you will appreciate the theory that all sounds can positively or negatively affect your environment, thus contributing to your positive emotional state or stress."

I made sure that no other comments were on the tips of their tongues and placed the flute back to my lips. I played a short melody. As I played the final note, no one spoke. Some nurses held their eyes closed. Marie then said, "That wasn't so bad."

After a discussion on how certain tones affect people and can set the theme and culture of the environment, I mentioned the squeaky chair I heard when I entered the unit. I said, " If it is true that music is a combination of sound and silence then some of your music is squeaky. How does that make you feel?"

The nurses began to comment that the squeaky chair was not contributing to a positive work environment. Together we looked at the perceived positive and negative sounds in their environment and questioned how these sounds were affecting both themselves and the seniors they served.

I turned to my initial ally in the room, Debbie, who had invited me to speak to the group. She stood up and announced, "So we are going to do a music project. We are going to spend a couple of days and assess the most stressful times of the day and then we are going to see if music can help you and the patients feel less stressed." There were no cheers or claps just a couple of nods and a change of topics as they finish their lunch.

The next day Debbie and I walked around the facility together making notes. We had some indicators as to what represented particularly stressful moments. These included escalation in sounds especially distressed sounds; activity in the hallways; and verbal comments such as "this is the worst part of the day." Not to our surprise the most stressful times were:

- the thirty minutes before each meal when staff were having to place out 150 trays of food
- when residents being transported to the dining rooms at the end of each hall
- when individuals needed help out of their bed or bath to be in time for their meal - more than staff ratios could support
- shift change
- evening bed time when the residents felt restless and often wandered the halls.
- After weeks of negotiation with the Chief Administrator, we finally reached an agreement to play music through the intercom system. We wanted to keep the music potent; therefore we wanted music just played at certain times of the day. If we played continuous music, it would no longer act as a theme song or trigger and would become less powerful. We played music for only thirty minutes each time. We then asked staff and residents what they thought and then made a few adjustments along the way.

One song we selected was an environmental piece. When it was played, one lady in the hall convinced herself she was looking for the waterfall and the crickets. We assured her that she did hear them and that we were going to turn it off soon. That song did not stay on our playlist.

There were also a couple of selections that annoyed some of the nursing staff, and so we made more adjustments. Although it is always difficult to please everyone, there is a way to find music that doesn't particularly offend. The results at the end were many unsolicited comments of how the unit felt more "serene, happy and less stressed." We used music to set the desired tone not just for the residents but for the staff as well.

If you have high levels of stress in your life with which you cannot cope, the problem may not be with you, but with the techniques that you use to manage it. Work can be a stressful environment and it can be tough to make it through a day without some kind of anxiety reducer. That is why so many people use music to ease their minds and help them get through the day. Studies show music can actually lower your heart rate and reduce stress for some people.[9] Can it reduce stress for anyone? Chances are that, yes it can. The key is finding the right music to do the right work.

Worksheet: Your Auditory Diet

Question	Tuned In Answer If this were to mean something, what could it mean?
What instruments calms you almost immediately?	
What instrument boost your mood quickly?	
What sounds at home do you perceive as negative?	
What sounds at home do you perceive as negative?	
Do you feel you can control some/ or many of the sounds in your work and/or home environment? what are the implications of this?	
If you could add more of one positive tone/sound to your environment what would it be?	

All worksheets are also downloadable at www.tuneintomusic.ca

Step Four: Establish Your Anchor Songs

How many of you with your significant others have "your song?" How many of you have a song that no matter what, when you hear it or sing it, it stands as your anthem?

Many of us have what I call "anchor songs." Anchor songs or theme songs help firmly fix us to an emotional state, luring us into action. Some very skilled persuaders, including political leaders, have found that theme songs could be their greatest ally to influence large groups of people—of course this has not always for the greater good, however the attempt to assist people to achieve a state of courageous brotherhood by helping them feel connected has had its benefits.

Movies and television programs attempt to use anchor songs all the time to hold your attention and set the emotional state desired for the scene. Oftentimes, the same piece of music will be used later in the program as a reminder or to demonstrate that an issue has been resolved.

Examples of this are all over T.V. shows—especially police shows and hospital or doctor shows. Music is the background for the most mundane of things—driving down the street, looking through binoculars, and identifying the drug used at a crime scene. Most important of all is the music background for the lab analysis. They do it all with music— building in the background to give us often a false sense of action and suspense. Music is a powerful persuader with the potential to take you just about anywhere.

While there are many commercial entities that have theme songs, I'm a huge proponent of personal anchor songs. These are songs that trigger memories very quickly and act as our personal anthems. An anchor song prepares our psyche and makes a moment often that much more meaningful.

Exercise: Select Your Anchor Song(s)

An anchor song becomes so ingrained that it anchors the listener to an emotional state immediately upon hearing it. There are a number of ways you can incorporate theme songs into your daily life.

Here are just a few. Choose a song (or an entire playlist) to anchor the following events:

- "first thing in the morning" song to anchor the tone of your home, giving you a sense of stability"
- "get ready for school" songs that motivates you for the day
- "mealtime with the family" songs that promotes socializing and a sense of comfort
- "study so I get an A" songs that helps you feel focused
- "relax after a stressful day" songs that takes you from feeling chaotic to calm in minutes
- "celebrating special holiday" songs that spark a
- the feeling I hope to achieve in the next 15 minutes

By now, you have identified much of your music from your history as well as your current listening habits. You likely have begun to hear music in a new way, not just something you passively let happen to you, but something you can actively choose to control.

I have just given you four ways in which you can find your music. While these exercises may seem simple, they can have a profound effect.

Carrie: A New Thought

For Carrie, a music teacher with twenty-five years of experience working in the public school system, using music now means doing something for her wellness, but it wasn't always like that.

I had been intimidated to speak to this hugely talented group of music educators and had questioned whether the concept of using music intentionally was even relevant to this already music savvy group. Carrie, the veteran teacher, asked if we could speak privately after the session. We sat with a couple of coffees and Carrie began to tell me her impressive resume. In addition to leading bands and choirs for twenty-five years, Carrie had been a lyric soprano travelling to Europe to work on many occasions. She loved to perform, conduct and teach students. Then she told me this:

"I'm telling you so much of my history because today is the first day I realized that although I use music daily I do not use music for myself. I do not use music to intentionally help me through difficult times. In fact, music has become something I share and learn and enjoy but not necessarily feed on myself."

Carrie found this subtle change of thinking quite profound and all that she required was a few strategies to bring music into the foreground for her wellness. She began to think about music in a way she had not considered before. She began to document her history with music and what she had done but added to that her feelings about it.

For the non-musician, the quest of bringing music into the foreground and using it with intention may look differently for someone with Carrie's experience. Carrie had all sorts of experience with music and was just missing the permission needed to use it in a different way that would help her in a way she wanted to be helped.

Take this book as permission to find your music and use it with greater intention to improve your wellness. I urge you to take the time, like Carrie did, to document your history, your feelings, your relationship to music. That is the best way I know of to be able to possess your own music, to use it causatively as opposed to simply react to it, to use it therapeutically with intention to help make your world a saner, happier place.

CHAPTER 5

Maximize Your Music

"I never wanted to be famous, I only wanted to be great."
Ray Charles

For over twenty years, I have been speaking to audiences about music therapy and the intentional use of music. Throughout North America both practices are increasingly recognized in hospitals, classrooms, and private residences. Over the course of my career, I have observed all the things I have said about music in this book: that it can boost mood, decrease stress, improve communication, and accomplish a whole host of miraculous and positive changes. I've seen so many miracles happen with music that they sometimes become routine. I expect these miracles to happen. And that has led me to believe, with absolute certainty that "Yes, music can do all these things."

Even more significant, music can tap into the best of us—our best memories, our best feelings, the parts of us that we may have forgotten. But what I love best about music is that it has the ability to remind us of the best parts of ourselves. That's why I've titled this chapter "Maximize your Music."

The point of this entire book is to first ignite you into action then to give you ideas about how, through music, you can take action using music to successfully achieve your goal. There are many ways to uplift your spirits—music just happens to be one very powerful way to do that.

Music brings out the best in anyone, and as you start applying the tips and techniques I've given you throughout this book, I want you to remember what you're shooting for: the very best that life has to offer. It is not just about using music intentionally, it is about using your life intentionally for good.

Scott: Live on a High Note

I want to tell you a story about a very special friend of mine, one who has always reminded me that music can trigger happiness and celebrate life. My friend was the epitome of positive attitude and he also taught me that we can all contribute something greater than ourselves if we want to. I am grateful I had an opportunity to meet him at a such a young age.

When Scott entered the grade eleven Physics class, everyone just blatantly stared at him. Scott had bright red hair, an incredibly small body, and was seated on a huge black wheelchair that looked too big for a boy his size. Scott was from the "special needs" class downstairs with other students who were rarely seen by the rest of the school. The special needs students would arrive in special buses after the regular buses had already left the school. Later in the day the special needs students would be picked up a little earlier than the regular students so there would be no chance for intermixing. To see someone like Scott walk, or rather roll into our regular class, was a new experience for all of us.

Scott's physical needs were such that he required an aide. The name of Scott's aide was Brian. Just one look at Brian, tall, blond and twenty-five, and it was a no-brainer. I moved over and made room for the two of them to sit at my table. Over the next year, I learned a lot about Scott (and Brian, who already had a pretty blonde girlfriend that he was thinking of marrying—sigh). Like many of the people with perceived deficits whom I have met over my lifetime, I could always count on Scott to be full of authentic joy and great humour each day. It quickly became apparent that what he lacked in physical abilities he made up for in above average intelligence and a great outlook on life.

Scott was a kid who loved going to church. He liked to sing and raise his hands up to God. I liked going to church with Scott because he worshipped through music with so much freedom and love. The music was lively and inspirational and matched how I had come to see Scott. He would always sing along with the music at the top of his lungs, and it didn't matter to anyone that he was out of tune. On a few Sundays, Brian's singing quartet would perform a special song, and Scott and I would wave to him from the balcony.

I finished grade eleven Physics with an "A," in large part thanks to Scott's tutoring. I looked forward to another class with Scott in grade twelve. During our second year in class together, Scott missed a lot of school and before Christmas he became quite sick. On Christmas Eve, Brian called me at home and said Scott had unexpectedly passed away after catching pneumonia. As I cried, Brian told me, "His little body fought as hard as it could, he just couldn't hold on any longer." He then went on to say, "Scott's dream was to be able to attend 'regular school.' He reached his dream."

That Christmas break I attended Scott's funeral. Brian's quartet sang and celebrated Scott. They kept the music upbeat and inspirational, just like Scott. It was the first time I experienced death, and I wasn't sure how to feel. But I did know that everything and everyone kept reminding me what Scott was all about—love and perseverance.

To this day when I hear the song, "Love Lift Us Up Where We Belong" I automatically think about Scott's tiny body, big brain, and bold heart. His life still rings through many people today, and really all it takes for me to lift myself up when I'm feeling a bit down is to think about Scott and sing a few bars of that song. I immediately remember to celebrate life, no matter what's in front of me. It gives me the bold courage to move on—even when sometimes I don't really want to.

Sam: Lead the Way

A few years after Scott's passing, another person was leading the way by living on a high note. This person taught me how to share his positive energy and optimism with others.

I was almost at the end of the road before I saw the looming grey building at the top of the hill. I had seen places like this on TV: a large multi-level grey building with winding hallways and floors beneath the surface no longer accessed except by maintenance people and ghosts. I lived just a few towns over and had no idea this place existed. It has since been demolished but in the early eighties it was very active. That day would be my first visit.

I nervously made my way into the stark lobby. After waiting barely a minute a man came around the corner in a relaxed friendly manner, a guitar slung across his shoulder.

"Hi, I'm Sam. You must be Jennifer," he said, "Come with me," motioning for me to follow him. "We have a little way to go so we better hurry as the group starts in twenty minutes." I picked up my bag and followed him. He chatted all the way, asking me about school and what area of town I was from.

He walked me through many doors and hallways until we arrived at a small room with a one-way mirror and cinder block walls. Adorning the walls were cheaply-framed pictures of generic-pink and faded- yellow flowers. No one else was in the room.

"Put your bags down here and follow me. We have to collect the team," Sam said with a smile that seemed to be a permanent fixture on his face.

As we walked down another hallway, he explained that every week he gathered the five individuals who would be a part of the group that day. He pushed open the double steel doors. I heard a lot of sounds, something in-between singing and talking. The voices echoed eerily off the walls. I recognized my own discomfort but Sam's steady pace and on-going chatter put me at ease. A few feet from the doorway was a small person with blonde curly hair and glasses lying on the floor against the wall. I could not gauge her age but was told later that the group members were in their twenties. She was hitting her head repeatedly against the wall.

Sam bent down, touched the girl's shoulder and said, "Hi Susan." She immediately stopped hitting her head. He whispered a few words into her ear and tickled her shoulder and she began to laugh. He walked into her room, found a small wheelchair, lifted her into it and asked me to push her while we sought out a few other members.

This scenario repeated four more times with Sam walking by a person who had not even noticed we were there until Sam gently touched a shoulder or knee to get their attention. Sam would help each of them to their feet or into a wheelchair. Soon we were a small group heading back through the winding halls to the group room.

Once we were gathered I helped Sam make a circle of chairs and wheelchairs. He instructed me to sit in the circle with everyone else. I nodded and felt somewhat more comfortable than I did before. I looked at all the individuals sitting around the room. They were different sizes and shapes.

Some wore glasses and others squinted. Many looked like mobility was not a prime concern. Some were not able to sit up properly and needed pillows to be reasonably comfortable. Visions of my friend Scott from high school in his wheelchair filled my head and I reflected on his words: "I am just so happy to be at regular school." I learned that everyone lived here together, but a school environment it was not.

Sam spoke to everyone like he did to me with firm direction, pleasant questions, and a smile. When you were with Sam, you felt well taken care of.

Once everyone was settled, he opened his guitar case and put the strap around the back of his neck. A quick tune, then a strum, and then a moment of silence. Heads lifted and their attention peaked. A small giggle escaped Susan. It was in the moment of the first few notes and chords that I saw a transformation in the small faces that just moments ago had held vacant stares, silence, or in Susan's case, the violence of hitting her head against the wall. Legs started to swing, heads started to bob, and chins went back. Mouths opened and sounds started to escape from a few patients. Some even sang the words while others tapped the tray on their wheelchair. Sam was still smiling and I realized my toes had started tapping. I had a smile plastered all over my face too.

Living in the positive means that you find a way to handle life's barriers. It certainly does not mean that you look at life through rose-colored glasses. But that experience with Sam has always reminded me that no matter what cards life deals you, take the high road. Look at life as something to be enjoyed, and never be afraid to find the music that can help you express that.

Create a Positive Auditory Diet

This last part is really a summation of all the work that we've done. As we journey into the last part of the book, I want you to reflect on your desired purpose for music. I have constantly asked you throughout: what do you want music to help you accomplish? Creating an auditory diet pulls together all the ideas I've presented to you throughout the book and puts them onto one healthy plate.

A good auditory diet can help you:
1. use music to help you handle adverse situations,
2. use music as a preventative tool and,
3. improve your quality of life

Like all healthy diets, variety is recommended. The critical factor when creating a healthy diet is to find the right combination of foods that help you reach your goals. Your auditory diet is no different. It involves some trial and error but at the end of the day it is about identifying what combination of sounds, silence, and music that works best for you.

What makes diets truly successful is sticking to them. It was during a trip with a dietician that I began to see the similarities between our daily diet and our auditory diet. We were hired to speak at the same set of conferences and during our off-hours we talked about our interests. By the end of our tour I had learned the perfect blend of carbohydrates and proteins for every meal and that a colourful plate was important for vitality and longevity. In a way, music also has different colours. They're called moods (you know, happy, sad, dark, etc.). The trick is to incorporate moods that suit your specific tastes. However, unlike nutrition there are no set guidelines for finding the perfect music plate. It's what your heart, mind, body, or soul needs in that moment for comfort, for inspiration, and for everything in between.

As we left for the first city, my new dietician friend and I settled into our seats on the plane. When the flight began you could hear the acceleration of the engine—that was normal. But then the sound almost stopped when the plane hit a certain altitude. The dietician next to me leaned over and said, "are the engines still working? I can't hear them."

Then the landing gear curled up back into its spot sounding like thunder in this older plane. The people in front of me jumped. We all sat in shocked silence for a moment and then many of us looked around carefully and began to laugh. Like our daily intake of food many of us don't pay attention to our auditory diet unless we digest something not quite right and hear something that is irritating or shocking. Luckily for us the plane was fine, just old.

When we see something we don't like, we can choose to close our eyes, but when we hear something we don't like, the sound coming into our ears is much more difficult to cover. Our auditory diet is difficult to control and therefore not something we spend a lot of time defining.

Society is also more visual than auditory, paying greater attention to what we see than to what we hear. The good news is that unlike most diets that are about eliminating or lessening certain foods - essentially being about losing something - our auditory diet works best when we add in something good and continue to add good things over long periods of time. It may not happen to everyone but sometimes people get sick and tired of music and stop listening. For each person it can be a different reason, and often the problem can be rectified by a change in auditory diet.

In a recent blog post, one author revealed he had become tired of music. The blogger went on to explain that he had a fairly exhaustive music collection and had listened to many of his albums over and over throughout his lifetime—well over thirty years. Not only had he eventually become tired of listening to music, he also found the addition of new music was no longer stimulating.

Responses to his post included those who were in total agreement, validating him by saying that they felt the same. Others diagnosed the blogger with everything from boredom to depression. Some even suggested he seek medical support. The blogger returned online and said "No, I can assure you I don't generally feel bored or depressed about the rest of my life, just music." After more dialogue the blogger came to his own personal conclusion that he felt he was suffering from music fatigue. He felt he just needed a break, and decided to spend his time on another activity.

After initially feeling concerned for the blogger, I realized that his statements were rational and insightful. Anything in our life that we use as entertainment or distraction can easily become something that we feel fatigue over, or grow out of, or need a break from once in a while. This is especially true if we are using music the same way all the time.

In this case, the blogger was clear that his process when listening to music meant moving from album to album, depending on his mood, listening from the first song to the last. He had enjoyed listening to music that way for over thirty years until his eventual fatigue. However, I didn't get the sense the blogger needed a break from music itself. He just needed a break from the way he was using music. He needed to change his approach.

Over the years there are certain sounds in my auditory diet that I really love—my dog snoring, people laughing, bamboo chimes on a summer's porch, blues music in the dark and Reggae music in the summer. These sounds are the perfect music mix to reflect what I value most in life: family, friends, and home.

A thoughtful, retired senior was feeling isolated at home after her husband passed away, she told me that one of her favourite sounds was children laughing. Her only grandchildren had moved away from the city and she missed their "mischief and giggles." After discussing how to access more of these happy sounds that trigger a happy response she mentioned there was a school a little further down the road. She normally did her walks early in the morning before many people were up. I made the simple suggestion that she move her walks to mid-day during the children's recess, to see if she felt the emotional lift that was lacking before.

Starting the following day she began her walk later in the morning with the goal to circle the school during recess. Later she mentioned how full her heart felt as she heard the sound of the children playing. We designed her auditory diet with the goal of feeling less isolated, and it worked.

An auditory diet will consist mostly of music, but don't neglect the non-music sounds in your life that bring you comfort, uplift your spirits, or just plain make you happy. They're as important as the songs you pick, sometimes even more important.

Strategies and Exercises to Maximize your Music

As you work on paying attention to your auditory diet, you will become more aware of the various purposes for the different music you choose. Subsequently, once you define your purposes for music, it will be easier to select the music you need to reach that desired purpose.

The following strategies and exercises are for marrying your purpose with your best auditory diet in order to achieve the change you desire.

Strategy 1: Music Memories

When you're constructing your personal soundtrack to build your auditory diet, remember that music is memorable. When you listen to music, feelings are associated with the song. Even if memories are not recovered, emotions and attitudes are—allowing people who can't even remember who they are from day-to-day remember something or someone they loved. Listening to music engages many areas of the brain in both hemispheres, which is why it can create brain activity when other methods, like conversation, cannot. When you are listening to your old albums, have you ever noticed your foot tapping on its own? That's not just because you like the music. It's because the portions of the brain which deal with rhythm and movement are so automated that it requires no conscious attention to move to a beat.

People have long known that music can trigger powerful recollections, but now brain-scan studies show us what is really happening and why when we use the right music we can actually help keep our memories in good working order. The part of the brain known as the medial pre-frontal cortex sits just behind the forehead. It's like a mechanical movie projector that shows what's happening in our minds. Petr Janata, a cognitive neuroscientist at University of California describes what music does.[1] He says that when a piece of familiar music matches an experience in our lives the listener experiences a mental movie that starts playing in our head. Memories flood back to us often in great detail. This information is important because music can therefore help us remember important events and people through the music that we associate with that event or person. So, identifying the music that triggers memories can be useful in helping to recall memories and will help keep those memories sharp.

Goerta: Remember Where I Came From

Nurses had to wheel ninety-two year old Goerta in to my therapy sessions. She always sat slumped over the tray of her wheelchair. Sometimes she was sleeping and sometimes she was hitting people as they walked too close to her. The nurses assured me that her family had insisted she attend every music therapy session because music had always been an important part of her life. Regardless of what song I sang, how soft or loud I sang it, whether it was a waltz or lullaby, or what instrument I used, Goerta continued to slump in her chair. Occasionally she took a moment to look up and create words that sounded like "hmph" while she flicked her wrist towards my face. I couldn't tell what Goerta disliked more—me or my music.

Several weeks later, a tall, middle-aged woman stood in the shadows of the room not making a sound. She stayed in one position for a half hour. As I closed the session she slowly walked over to Goerta's wheelchair where Goerta slumped to the side. The unknown woman crouched down, and looked up into her eyes. Goerta made no movement. The tall stranger began to sing in a language foreign to me.

After a few lines of the song Goerta lifted her head slightly. She had tears in her eyes as did her singing companion. The two of them finished the song together. This was the first time I heard Georta's voice. The song came to a close and the two women clutched hands fervently. The stranger looked at me and said, "I never thought to sing to my mom. This is the first time we have connected in four years." One month later, I received a letter from Russia, with the words (and phonetic spelling) along with the transcribed music of two folk songs that Goerta might like to hear. I learned them, and without fail, Goerta would brighten up and sing many of the words and melodies that were familiar to her when I sang them.

Exercise:
Create Your Personal Soundtrack

Bring together the following resources: a pen and paper, a copy of the personal soundtrack form downloadable from www.tuneintomusic.ca

1. Take a few moments to settle your mind, close your eyes, and slow your breath.

2. Begin to imagine yourself as a very young person (sometimes looking at pictures of yourself when you were young before closing your eyes will help you visualize that time in your life more easily).

3. As you think of yourself at that young age begin to open your ears and think about the positive sounds, silences, and music that were in your life at that time.

4. When these sounds become almost truly audible, open your eyes and start documenting these memories. Capture as many music memories from your childhood as you can.

5. Continue with your memories through each major stage of your life starting with your earliest childhood memories and finishing with your current music memories.

6. This activity will take a minimum of one hour to complete and will most likely be something that you come back to time and time again as you remember music that has been important to you throughout your lifetime.

Strategy #2: Bring Music to the Foreground

All music influences us in some way. Background music definitely has its place in our life as we accomplish other important tasks. It sets the mood for a party, banishes silence, comforts us when we are alone, and makes the horror movie unbearable. But it can be so much more.

If music has demonstrated such potency, how can we access its power in our daily lives and use it for our personal gain? It all comes down to bringing music into the foreground. Music is ever-present and accessible, yet it often accompanies something else we are doing. To bring music upfront means to use music directly for a purpose. To listen to it consciously and with intention.

Tory: Finds a Voice

For Tory, bringing music into the foreground meant using music to find her lost voice. Local Child and Family Services informed me that they had a small, quiet, two- year-old girl they wanted me to meet. They went on to tell me a very sad story of how she had sustained a serious injury at the hands of her dad when she was less than a year old. Since then, she communicated little emotion. Her aunt informed us that at one time, she had been a great giggler. When she was removed from her family home, she could no longer sit up and did little more than hold a vacant stare. She was placed in a loving foster care environment. The foster mother worried she had a little girl that would never improve.

All you could see was the mass of blonde curls at the top of Tory's head. Her chin rested on her chest as she reclined slightly in a soft cradle seat that was specially designed for her. She was strapped in so she would not just crumple to the floor. Foster mom looked at me quizzically when I asked that Tory be lifted up on to the dining room table. "I want to be able to sit in a chair with my guitar and look up at her," I responded.

I pulled a chair up to the table and looked into Tory's remarkable blue eyes. I began to sing a familiar lullaby. Over the next several minutes, I blended her name into the lyrics. At the sound of her name, I saw a light behind her eyes for the first time. Contact!

Foster mom and I nodded to each other and she gave a slight smile. She sat on the couch on the other side of the room, watching.

Over the next year, with the help of Tory's foster mom, we developed a program rooted in music that Tory would participate in every day. I visited once a week and Foster mom did the program on the other days in the week. The goal was to offer music that had a diversity of sounds, pitches, melodies and speed to actively engage her brain as much as possible. Although Tory could watch TV with music or listen to the radio, we wanted as much live music as possible and it seemed she really wanted that too. It was the twinkle that sparkled in her eye that gave her away. It was the tell-tale sign that music was working for her.

It took a year for Tory to identify with a sound or instrument. And then it happened. Near Tory's fourth birthday she let out a giggle. I played the wrong note by accident one day and then mocked myself in the song singing in a higher pitch that was even more out of tune. That's when I got the giggle.

Over the years, Tory had learned the songs as they were intended, and when she heard them all mixed up it touched her funny bone. Bringing music upfront in Tory's life helped her learn to giggle again. Her aunt was right—she had the most delightful giggle and I was very fortunate to hear it many times after that.

Exercise: Create the Right Kit

In order to bring music upfront and into the foreground, it is important to ensure that your music preferences are accessible and in a form that you can easily retrieve when you need it.

I remember when I was in elementary school, I would go to my friend's house because they had the better stereo to play records on. Then in middle school it was all the rage to have a portable cassette player. Then in high school, you envied the kids who had a Walkman (a portable CD player). Then after my children were born iPods became the "in" thing! It seems like technology keeps changing so fast. I honestly hardly listen to the radio unless it is in the car. Once in a while I'll pop a CD in my stereo, but it's very rare nowadays. I use my phone to access my music since the sound quality is surprisingly good.

What do you use to listen to your music?

It is important to ensure your music is accessible for when you need it most. It is important that you have a medium in which to listen and a selection of listening music. Include positive sounds and in some cases time for silence.

In order to ensure you have what you need when you need it I recommend you:

1. Talk with your friends and ask them what their favourite way of listening to music is.

2. Invest in the medium that works best for you. Do not sacrifice quality if at all possible. Different earphones have different qualities. Take time to do online research, inquire at electronics stores, and speak with your friends before making your music medium choice. Quality sound enhances the healing process.

3. Ensure you have everything you prefer to listen to for the different goals in your life. Continue to collect music that captures your attention and heart.

Strategy #3: Music Acts Like a Drug

As discussed in part two, music can fill your mind with many happy chemicals. Dr. Daniel Levitin has proven that listening to music releases certain chemicals in the brain.[2] Dopamine, a "feel-good hormone" is released every time you listen to music you like. Listening to music with someone else can also release prolactin, a hormone that bonds people together. And if you sing together? You release oxytocin, which causes feelings of trust.

You can choose music to match or change your emotional state. You can choose music to become more relaxed or to motivate you for a challenging activity. Music is as powerful as some drugs. Music affects certain chemicals which relay information in our mind. Drugs work in a similar way except they make your brain lazy and convince it to stop making its own chemicals. Introducing music can increase levels of some chemicals including those I listed above as well as serotonin (regulator of mood, appetite and sleep). In addition certain music lowers heart rate, blood pressure, and muscle tension.

540 People: a Change in Perception

People have different emotional reactions to the same music. A random sample of 540 Spanish consumers (aged fifteen to sixty-five) were played a series of radio advertisements for a fictitious mineral water.[3] Each advertisement used a different style of music in the background, aimed at evoking a different emotion. The listener's perceptions were measured by looking at their emotional reaction to the advertisement and then how they perceived the brand of the water.

One group listened to the advertisement with no music. The other groups had various kinds of emotional music attached to the ad. The average score for "emotional reaction generated" among the consumers was significantly higher for the versions of the advertisement with music accompaniment than the one without any music. The average score was also significantly higher when using a song the listener knew and loved. Although the speaking voice for the advertisement never changed, the responses to the tone of voice depended on what music was playing behind the speaking voice. When faster and more grandiose music was used the listeners thought the speaking voice seemed happier, more restless, excitable, impatient, jovial, sporty, enthusiastic, and daring than in the second version (even though it was the same voice at the same speed). On the contrary, the people who listened to the music version that was slower and more subdued found the person speaking to be calmer, more relaxed, patient, delicate, understanding, disciplined, mature and trustworthy. The brand of the product followed a similar line to the emotions the person felt as they listened to the advertisement.

What we listen to not only affects our mood but it also seems to affect our greater perception on the world. This is important to consider when we select music to improve our emotional state.

Exercise: Assess Your Auditory Diet

Your auditory diet is a combination of what is being heard and how often it is heard.

1. After completing your personal soundtrack downloadable from the www.tuneintomusic.ca website you will then want to identify your current listening habits, also available on my site.

2. Give yourself time to review the data above, asking yourself repeatedly what your responses could mean. I highly recommend reviewing with someone who knows you well and that you trust.

3. When you have identified your current auditory diet begin to set some goals around your desired emotional state.

4. Again review your personal soundtrack and find the time in your life and the associated music that triggered that desired emotional state.

5. Put together a playlist, even if it is just one, two or three songs to start.

6. Take a few moments to turn the music on and see if it sparks your desired emotional state. Remember this will involve some trial and error but at the end of the day it is about identifying what combination of sounds, silence, and music that works best for you to reach the desired emotional state you want for: when you arrive at work, when you arrive at home, when you are at the gym, when you are setting the morning tone of your home, or when you are going to sleep at night.

Strategy #4: Use Music with Intention

While the entire book really is about using music intentionally, by now you know what it means to use music with intention, with purpose, with awareness of what you want it to do. Lacking intention means removing meaning and direction. Here I want to council you to be as specific as you can when defining your purpose with music. For example, choose music to boost your immune system. Or choose it to help you take your mind off of the three-in-the-afternoon blues when all you want to do is eat. Then allow the music to do what you want it to do—help keep you healthy or help you indulge in the pleasure of music instead of food. Music reduces stress by reducing cortisol levels, a chemical in your brain that causes you to feel stress in the first place. Are you wondering if your favourite music is helping your health? Good questions to ask are: Does this music make me feel more anxious? Self-pitying? Uncomfortable? If you answer yes to questions like that, then you may want to try something new.

The answer to boosting your mood, decreasing your stress, calming your staff or motivating your clients comes down to setting your intention. Definitions of intention include the words "to have in mind a purpose or plan, to direct the mind, to aim." Lacking intention therefore means to stray away from meaning and goals.

Setting your intention for music will be, interestingly enough, a non-music goal. It could include but not be limited to such items as: increase confidence, decrease stress, or feel more connected with others. It could be to achieve better health or physical fitness or to spend more quality time with loved ones. Intentions can be generalized, but the more specific your intention, the more easily you can identify how you can help yourself achieve that goal with music. The point here is that the goal has to be named before you can work to accomplish it.

My Goal: Improve the Tone of my Home

When my children were five and six, I thought I was going to lose my mind. Initially, I was so excited. That was the year both kids would be in school, and I would be able to spend my days happily at work and then come home, make a happy dinner, hug my children, and tuck them in at night. As it turned out, by dinner-time, I found myself exhausted from being up so early in order to organize my home each day.

Our home "stress time" seemed to always be in the morning. My husband worked late and therefore started work late, leaving the morning routine with the children up to me to manage solo. My kids were really active in the morning. They both have strong personalities. My daughter Braedan lives joy out to the fullest every day. She has no internal monologue, so there is very little going on in her life that you do not know about. My son Merrick is a doer and has a very defined way of doing things. He has an order and he does not like chaos. Three different personalities and procedures working together in the same space working towards the same common goal sometimes felt very chaotic.

Mornings at one time were my favourite time of day, but it was getting to the point where I dreaded mornings. I began to feel guilty because by the time the kids got on the bus, we did not have a good farewell. I needed help. As usual, it took me awhile to remember my greatest resource—music. Could it possibly work?

Even though I use music often, I still have moments where I question its validity. Time and time again, however, I find that it is not music that isn't working. It's the implementation. I gave some thought to what I could try. It would mean losing some more sleep, but I decided it was worth it.

The next morning I woke up forty-five minutes before the kids and snuck downstairs to the living room that adjoined to our kitchen. I turned on the soothing classical music I chose the night before. Even though I was very tired, I felt the room lift as soon as I turned on the music. I noticed myself take a deep, calming breath. Then I went into the kitchen and set up the table with the breakfast supplies. I went back upstairs and started getting ready for the day. I could hear the music. After some time, I heard one of the children get up and go downstairs. They didn't come back up and they didn't turn on the TV (or ask if they could).

Then the second door opened, this time my daughter got up and yelled up the stairs, "Mom! The music is on." I smiled. I waited for them music to turn off, but they didn't. I heard some dishes rustling at the table and

I knew they were having their cereal. By the time they were back upstairs, I was ready to go and could just monitor their getting-ready process.

I am not saying the house was quiet—it wasn't. We still talked; we still slammed the occasional closet door but there was definitely a difference. There was a calming, intentional presence in the home that was not there previously. I didn't get up every morning and prepare the music context in my house but whenever I did, I noticed a similar difference. We continue this ritual to this day and now the kids, who are almost ready to leave for college, actively participate in choosing the music we listen to in the morning.

I had little music in my home growing up. When my parents split my mom had to take two jobs in order to support us and pay the mortgage. She was always so worried. We didn't go to daycare—we were "latchkey kids." We had to stay at home with the doors locked.

Most days I would walk home with friends after school, take my key from around my neck, open the door, lock it immediately, and then call my mom. I always felt a little nervous. Sometimes I would open the back door and I would hear music playing quietly on the radio. That's when I knew my mom was home. I was safe. Neither one of us figured out that if she left the radio on all day—or even used a timer to turn it on—I may have felt that same sense of safety.

Using music intentionally is critical if we hope to achieve our goals whether it be to set a tone of connection and calm at home or to give children the sense of security they need. As you use music with greater intention I am certain you will continue to find new music that might turn into positive memories and anchor songs that will support you through whatever life throws your way.

Exercise: Set Intentional Goals

Outside of using music for entertainment what more can music do for you? The answer is simple—almost anything you want it to. It comes down to using music intentionally.

The first question is "what do you need?" This is not always an easy question to answer. Take a moment to choose just one area that you are hoping to affect. Do you want to feel less stressed, more connected, more focused, or remember a meaningful person in your life?

The key to intentionally use your music is to first address what you use it for. Once you do that you can choose your music with a greater consciousness.

Strategy #5: Preferences Matter

The final guideline is perhaps the most important as it relates to how you choose your music preferences. Remember how I so carefully chose the music to help me through my daughter's birth, but when I got to the actual event, the music was all wrong?

Keep in mind that although you like the music you choose for whatever purpose, it is important to evaluate whether you are getting the results you want from it or not. If you choose a piece of music that makes you feel worse, then perhaps you need to re-address your music. Choosing the right music for the right time is key to successfully using music therapy techniques to enhance your life. But do know that sometimes music will help you in ways you weren't expecting and all the planning in the world can't prepare you for what you really need.

Mcdonald Family: Jingle Bells

The Mcdonald family thought they were choosing just the right music until they heard it. This wonderful family spent every Christmas together. When the matriarch of the family was in the hospital, the entire family came to visit. Sharon Mcdonald, the head of the family, had always been close to each of her four children. Even after they were grown they all continued to live near each other and visited regularly.

Now in the hospital for Christmas, Sharon always had at least one family member by her side, if not two. When you walked past their door, the room was regularly filled with animated voices and laughter. I first met them a week before Christmas. I was walking to another patient's room when Sharon's son ran up to me and asked if I would come into their room for a moment. As I entered I was greeted by four other smiling faces. Each person had a bit of red in their hair, and it was easy to tell they were related. In the centre was Sharon. She lifted her hands and welcomed me with a two handed shake.

Then she said, "Christmas is a very important time for our family. We would be grateful if you would sing some of our favourite songs."

I agreed. Before I started everyone was lively and cheerful. I sat down amidst the group and pulled out my guitar. Sharon said, "Do you know Silent Night?" I began to play the familiar waltz. Everyone sang along and tears started to come down some faces. Sharon looked at everyone in the room and continued to smile.

When the song was over Sharon said, "That was just lovely, everyone. Thank you. The greatest gift you could give me is all being here today just a few days before Christmas. Hearing you all sing like that takes me away from the hospital and reminds me of all the Christmases we have been lucky to have together."

She then turned to me and said, "Jennifer, I think we need a song that we won't cry to this time. How about 'Jingle Bells'?"

I played my liveliest strum and opened into the first verse, "Dashing through the snow," I didn't even make it to the chorus when the entire room stopped singing and were crying more than they were before. The Christmas music, although the most suitable choice, was reminding the family more about what they wouldn't have this Christmas (their mom at home) than what they did have. I slowed the music down and was about to stop when Sharon started laughing. And soon everyone else was laughing with her. "I guess it doesn't matter what we sing I guess we are needing the music to help us cry."

Music can positively and negatively trigger our feelings and memories. When we choose our music intentionally, amazing things can happen. Our choices are critical when finding the right music for the right moment and for the right purpose. However sometimes, as Sharon recognized, the music can help you understand what you truly need in a moment more than anything else can.

Exercise: Identify Your Preferences

Your preferences are your greatest triggers to snap you into the mood you want to be in, but first we have to identify our preferences. In order to do that we have several considerations: style preferences, tempo preferences and timbre preferences.

Style preferences are often one of the easiest markers of music preferences. This is the kind of music we like. From classical to country, there are definite styles that we gravitate towards. It is fun as well as important to recognize what your style preferences are, but always leave yourself open to surprises. The activity forms on www. tuneintomusic.ca will help you begin to address the styles you most gravitate towards.

Your *tempo preferences* vary more often each day. The tempo of a song we like in the morning is often different than the speed of songs we like in the afternoon or just before we go to bed. When selecting a song for a party we often think of tempo first and select what we perceive is upbeat or relaxing depending the mood we want to evoke.

Finally there is your *timbre preferences*. Every instrument or voice carries with it its' unique timbre. All timbres attract or repel the person who hears it.

Once you have addressed your music preferences, perhaps even documenting them you may begin to see patterns to your day, week, month or experiences.

Use these preferences to then highlight your key anchor songs. An anchor song becomes so ingrained that it anchors an emotional state immediately upon hearing it. There are a number of ways you can incorporate theme songs into your daily life.

Choose a song (or an entire playlist) to trigger the events in your life you want to affect—your favourite song to wake up to, what you go to work to, and the one song that reminds you of the one you love.

Of course the above exercises will need to be repeated many times, and in some cases frequently as we are constantly going through new experiences that trigger new music and old music memories. What affects us today may not affect us tomorrow. That's the beautiful part of being a human being. You just need to help yourself become aware of what does affect you so that you can use that knowledge for the better—to take you to where you want to go.

As I spent time honing the process to maximize your music, I hope my goal has been realized: to create a usable guide so that anyone can benefit from the amazing effects music can create in your lives.

To use music effectively does take a commitment to be more mindful of how music affects you in various situations. It takes perseverance to discover the right music for the right situation. Above all, it takes a sense of adventure. Music can help you tap into your most creative self. It's power is almost incomprehensible because it is so simple a solution to many of life's difficulties.

So as you TUNE IN to your music, may you find the peace, the joy, the laughter, and even sometimes the tears, that I have found with my music.

Strategy #6: Find New Music

Finding new music can help you discover new things about yourself. Going to a concert, hearing an album or even just one song may introduce you to music that resonates so strongly that you will need to incorporate that music into your life soundtrack. I remember hearing Dad say during one of his infrequent visits that he loved Willie Nelson. Up to that point I didn't know Dad very well. When he mentioned that Willie Nelson was one of the few musicians who "knew how to sing a story," it caught me off guard. When I heard Willie Nelson's voice I winced at his crackling voice.

From that day forward, I began to listen more to Willie's stories and less to his tone of voice. This association, however small, helped me feel more connected to Dad when he wasn't around. To this day, every time I listen to or sing a Willie Nelson tune I think of Dad in a positive way.

One very special, meaningful moment was when I had an opportunity to attend an intimate concert with Willie Nelson. His voice no longer seemed crackly. In fact, it was beautiful. With tears running down my cheeks and goosebumps on my arms, I heard a man who certainly knew how to communicate love, encouragement, and heartbreak through song. He's obviously now part of my life's soundtrack.

One of the easiest ways to expand your playlist is to find out what some of your closest friends and family are listening to. The music that has captured their hearts is worth looking into. There is something about the way those particular musicians use their voices, put their lyrics together, and phrase their words that speaks uniquely to your friends. Perhaps when you understand and interact with the music of your good friends, you too will find a deeper connection to their music and to them.

Some of the greatest gifts I have received are from my friends who say "I heard this song and it made me think of you." In this way, I have been introduced to some incredible musicians that I otherwise would not have learned about. I am thankful these incredible people are in my life and are helping me to forever be expanding my music horizons.

Darcy: Broken Free

The strong effects music can create never cease to amaze me. Darcy, an attendee during one of my workshops on using music and sound for better health, came up to me at the end of our workshop. Earlier in the day we had addressed the sounds in our environment and how they affect us and had moved on to the next assignment—creating a playlist for work. I noticed that Darcy was having a difficult time with the second assignment.

When she approached me after class, I had a feeling that this was going to be intense and personal. She waited until the class dispersed, and then said, "Jennifer, I want to do the right thing. I work with teenaged girls, all of whom are coping with some pretty tough life experiences—experiences young girls should not have had to go through. Many are depressed and most are very nervous and anxious. We use music as a mood-shifter around the house and one type of music that seems to work best with the girls is soothing classical music for relaxation. My problem is that I have to remove myself from the room when that music is played." She fidgeted with her hands and looked me in the eyes "You see, classical music was played by my abuser while I was locked in my room."

Darcy's experience makes sense. There is a definite relationship with one's familiarity with a piece of music and the emotions it elicits. In one study, half of participants were played twelve random musical excerpts one time, and rated their emotions after each piece. The other half of the participants listened to twelve random excerpts five times, and started their ratings on the third repetition. Participants who listened to the excerpts five times rated their emotions with higher intensity than the participants who listened to them only once.[4] Preferences and familiarity continue to be linked to the emotions experienced by the listener.

Darcy continued, "I have done years of counseling, and feel I have broken free from his clutches. Now, I see myself as a healthy, married mom of four and I love my job. I even forgave my abuser years ago, but when I hear the music I feel like I am being abused all over again."

I admired this woman standing in front of me more than I can tell you. She was willing to impose the most traumatic images in her mind in order for others to feel soothed. There must be an alternative to not being able to hear classical music ever again. Avoiding classical music had seemed to be the best alternative to Darcy until she realized that she had to think of others. For Darcy, it was time to get practical and she wanted to do what was best for the girls with whom she worked.

Starting with the premise that the music that inspires us is the music that can motivate us and the music that relaxes us is music that soothes us, we just have to notice how we are affected by music to find the music that will relax and motivate us.

Over the course of several weeks of trial and error, Darcy created several playlists. She found music—some classical pieces even—that worked for both her and for her girls. When she played it in the house, she found it refreshing and the girls were less anxious—the all-around desired effect.

Darcy's story shows us that sometimes we already realize how music affects us, enough so that we change our behavior to accommodate this affect. Darcy's case is pretty extreme so the effect was hard to miss, but, once again, I am struck by how easy it is to use music positively if we are fully aware of what we're trying to accomplish.

Exercise: Create Purposeful Playlists

Technology has changed enough over the last decade to allow us to take our entire music library with us and to arrange it into playlists for particular purposes. Because music can now be "on demand," when you need support you have the choice of putting on the playlist that will help you achieve what you need at that moment.

Putting together playlists can be quite daunting for many, especially when people see this endeavor as one that takes time and money both of which may be unavailable. To prepare "Purposeful Playlists" try doing a little bit at a time. A "Playlist for Energy: Sports Performance" might simply be a matter of listening to songs on the radio and noticing how your body responds. If you hear a bright peppy song as you drive, it will most likely spark a similar reaction during an upcoming workout. Songs generally range in length from three to five minutes. By selecting six to eight songs, you can easily have a thirty-minute playlist that inspires and motivates you to an energetic workout.

By changing frequencies, tempo and music tones our entire being is affected. On a cold winter day, with my imagination flowing and with my eyes closed, just listening to music all by myself can transport me to a warmer climate and ultimate relaxation. In my mind, I sip my first margarita and mellow out while listening to the slow, melodic lapping of the waves on the beach. Just like the soothing nature of a hypnotic voice, music can put us to sleep or wake us up with changes in pitch. Having our playlists accessible at our fingertips can provide the feeling we need in the moment.

Strategy #7: Sing, Drum, Make Music

Some studies have shown that singing can even surpass the effects of yoga on your heart rate, breathing and general well-being. It has also been shown to be a helpful treatment for depression, anxiety and fatigue. When it comes to actually producing the best sound, your breath has to come from your diaphragm. You need to be sitting or standing straight, with relaxed shoulders, neck and face muscles, pushing the air up through your vocal cords into your facial cavity. Some are able to do this more naturally than others. The human voice is the first and most basic musical instrument. It doesn't cost a thing, one reason, perhaps, for the amazing vocal virtuosity that has come out of impoverished communities from Soweto to Wales to the Mississippi Delta. You don't have to be an opera singer or pop star to have fun with your own instrument. Read on for some suggestions to get you singing and feeling healthy.

Singing is a healthy activity. There is singing alone in the shower, singing around the campfire, getting up at karaoke, singing in a church choir, and performing in the community. For most singing is a social event, involving groups of people sharing melodies, lyrics, rhythms and each other's company.

Singing acts as a bond, which unites people in a common purpose. We have heard countless stories of how singing has lifted spirits during difficult times and made long voyages bearable. In our modern world of electronics, making music together seems to be happening less and less. It seems we only wait for special occasions. But science is clear, that people experience an increase in their perceived mental health when they sing with others. It also revealed significantly reduced anxiety and depression scores.[5]

Research has not only cemented previous studies that pointed to an increase in health benefits from community singing programs, but also demonstrated that singing programs are cheap healthcare. But just as you learned earlier in this book singing is not the only form of music making that can make a difference.   I had the experience of traveling to a remote village in Africa with a small team, a few drums, and percussion instruments. The children in the village had very little exposure to such instruments and immediately gravitated to them—rhythm has no language barrier, and oh, the rhythms from Africa.

The sessions were physical and energetic. It did not take long for the adults to join in. Although my favourite part of a drum circle continues to be the non-verbal sense of community it creates amongst friends, family and strangers we now know that drum circles and group music making can do so much more. Group drumming alters neuroendocrine and immunologic measurements in the participants—this means a boost to your immune system, which helps you be sick less often. Dr. Bittman found that group drumming strengthened the immune system by increasing Natural Killer (NK) cell activity.[6] It also showed less human stress response on the genomic level, not just reducing but reversing nineteen genetic switches that turn on the stress response believed responsible in the development of common diseases. Drumming was chosen for this study because percussion activities require little musical training or experience. Drumming and playing other percussion instruments is easy to catch on to. However, playing musical instruments also offer the same benefit of singing or drumming. According to a study published by the American Psychological Association, playing an instrument as a child keeps the mind sharper as we age.[7] There are benefits to starting an instrument in your later years, too. Music-making is linked to a number of health benefits for older adults including much of the reasons we have spoken about in this book. Making music can lower blood pressure, decrease heart rate, reduce stress, and lessen anxiety and depression. Anyone, regardless of age, ability, or affluence, can make music and benefit from it.

Exercise: Try Something New

If you're feeling stuck or in a funk then it may be time to do a pattern interrupt and there is nothing more cost effective or efficient than adding in new music to your auditory diet. It could be as simple as changing your radio station for a day or looking through the local community newspapers to register for a new music class. We often hear in sports medicine how beneficial it can be to shake things up in your routine –well your music making is no different.

Group lessons can take your experience to a whole new level. Jordan Metzl, a sports medicine physician at the Hospital for Special Surgery in New York says "Trying something new that shakes up your routine can really give you a fresh perspective and get you excited." [8]

Strategy #8: Boost Your Physical Performance

The body of research on workout music has swelled considerably, helping psychologists refine their ideas about why exercise and music are such an effective pairing for so many people. It seems that music distracts people from pain and fatigue, elevates mood, increases endurance, reduces perceived effort and may even promote metabolic efficiency. When listening to music, people perform farther, longer, and faster than usual—often without realizing it. In a 2012 review of the research, Costas Karageorghis of Brunel University in London, one of the world's leading experts on the psychology of exercise music, wrote that one could think of music as a legal performance-enhancing drug. In truth, it looks like music can boost your athletic performance by 15 percent! There's more to it than distraction, music makes people less aware of their exertion. The music seems to propel them forward helping them gain maximum benefit.[9]

Some psychologists have suggested that people have an innate preference for rhythms that are equivalent to 120 beats per minute (bpm), or two beats per second. When asked to tap their fingers or walk, many people unconsciously settle into a rhythm of about 120 bpm. An analysis of more than 74,000 popular songs produced between 1960 and 1990 have 120 bpm as the most prevalent pulse. When running on a treadmill, however, most people seem to favor music around 160 bpm. Websites and smartphone apps such as Songza and jog.fm help people match the tempo of their workout music to their running pace, recommending songs as fast as 180 bpm for a seven-minute mile, for example.

The rhythm of your workout music stimulates the motor area of the brain aiding in your movements and keeping them steady. This leads to a sense of greater efficiency since keeping a steady pace is easier on our bodies than fluctuating through the workout.[10]

Exercise: Boost Your Workout

Want to complete your first race? Use a playlist that induces Inspiration

Want to improve your cadence? It's all about the the right rhythm

Want to improve your power/strength? It's all about that bass

Want to be less lonely when you run? Load tunes onto your MP3 that are familiar and evokes many memories from your past

Need to change your outlook? Construct a playlist that evokes the feeling you want to have

Strategy #9: Get Music Back in Every School

In the introduction, I noted that music programs in schools are being cut because of budget constraints. Somehow, the logic goes, music is "extra" thus it shouldn't be funded. It pains me that we must fight to have the arts in school because the arts are thought of as fringe and not fundamental. Even with all the research that shows the vital part music can play in productivity, music is still considered "just music." Even though it seems there is no other activity in the world that works the brain harder, music is still being cut from schools.

In the sometimes harsh reality of limited budgets, the inclusion of the arts in every student's education is at risk. However, I do find myself questioning if it is just budget constraints that are putting our music programs in jeopardy or is there a lack of belief that music truly matters in the big picture? I believe music programs in school help our kids and communities be better—at pretty much everything.

Here are my top 3 reasons why music should be in every school:

1. *To foster connection and bridge culture and economic differences.* Although we have more instant access to our friends and family via technology there tends be a lack of connection that can only come with human to human contact working and being creative together. Music is a celebration of who we are and an exploration into our diversity. If we truly value this and believe that it is a strong component of our social fabric then music can celebrate these differences in a non-threatening, positive way. Music gives us an opportunity to gain a wider perspective on cultural history and backgrounds by being exposed to centuries of rich heritage.

"Music is a magical gift we must nourish and cultivate in our children, especially now as scientific evidence proves that an education in the arts makes better math and science students, enhances spatial intelligence in newborns, and let's not forget that the arts are a compelling solution to teen violence, certainly not the cause of it!" Michael Greene, Recording Academy President and CEO at the 42nd Annual Grammy Awards, February 2000.

2. ***To develop other academic skills.*** Music skills are proven to transfer over to study skills, communication skills, and cognitive skills; in other words, it is useful in every part of the curriculum. Music, when done with the right intention, is able to assist all children regardless of age or abilities, abolishing another potential societal gap. Aside from the social benefits, students in high school music programs have higher test scores and cognitive development. A U.S. Department of Education study found that those who reported consistent involvement in music programs during school years show significantly higher levels of mathematics proficiency by grade 12—regardless of students' socioeconomic status. Additionally, students who learn music develop a greater ability to learn a new language.[11]

3. ***To give students the opportunity to contribute to something greater than themselves.*** Each of us wants our children to feel successful in school, successful in employment, and successful in the social structures through which they participate. Music gives an opportunity to reach out to others, participate in a joint experience and then share….share with the audience, share with their cohort, share with parents who support them, share with the teachers that help them learn and share with the community that pays the taxes to ensure students receive life-giving education. Music gives something back and allows the listener to feel rewarded for their contribution in making it happen. Music is a two way communication that can make all people feel connected.

"Music is about communication, creativity, and cooperation, and by studying music in school, students have the opportunity to build on these skills, enrich their lives, and experience the world from a new perspective."
Bill Clinton, former President, United States of America

Exercise: Considerations to Maximize Music in Classrooms

We know that music can do:

1. Relax the mind and lower stress levels.[12]

2. Stimulate creativity by increasing blood and oxygen flow to the brain, helping the learner go from sleepy brain to teachable brain.[13]

3. Create a clear passage to long-term memory.[14]

4. Change an individual's emotional state[15]

Let's take this information and translate it for the classroom context. In order to Maximize our Music at school use these considerations:

1. The music we use, and how we respond to the music in our life is unique to everyone regardless of our age, ability or affluence. It absolutely depends on each person's preference and each person's preference depends on their musical histories, interests, age, ability and personal interests.

2. Classrooms may receive budgets to purchase new music-based resources; however they often do not get a budget to research what resources (and perhaps training) would be best for their specific needs. All classrooms are unique and all teachers' skill sets are unique. It is important to purchase resources that will be used on a regular basis and support your desired learning goals. Before spending too much money (instruments are expensive) speak to a music specialist and ensure you are getting the best for you and your school.

3. Do not have music playing all day. Use music intentionally at specific times of day. Select quiet, organizing music to use in the background as children enter the classroom. This creates a non-verbal message of intention to become more quiet and organized for the school day. Select short pieces of songs (one to two minutes) to indicate what is next: reading time, lunch, getting ready for gym. The teacher may have to say (for the first few days) what activity they are getting ready for but afterwards the music with speak to the students and inform them what's next, just like a TV theme song.

4. And finally, remember silence provides a pocket of space in which the sound just heard can be processed and consciously responded to. It is the listener's opportunity to react and give something in return. Silence can often be the reboot our brain needs to prepare for the next thing.

Strategy 10: The Economics of Using Music at Work

Nearly half of all workers suffer from moderate to severe stress while on the job, according to a recent survey. And 66 percent of employees report that they have difficulty focusing on tasks at work because of stress. Stress has been called the "health epidemic of the 21st century" by the World Health Organization and it costs American businesses up to $300 billion a year.[16]

But there are ways to reduce stress's daunting, pervasive impact on human lives and companies' bottom line. A survey of 2,500 employees by ComPsych, a provider of employee assistance programs (EAPs), highlights the problem. In addition to the challenges related to focus at work, employees also said that stress was responsible for errors and/or missed deadlines (21 percent), trouble getting along with co-workers/superiors (15.5 percent), missed days (14.9 percent) and lateness (14.4 percent).[17]

I like to say my life is full—not busy. Busy sounds negative to me, whereas full—well it sounds full. However full also means that there is no more room and that is not what I want for my day or week either. What I am always on the hunt for is a way to be more organized and more efficient in what I do, so I can create the margin required for the unexpected, hopefully some extra fun in the week. Here is how you can use music to boost your productivity, and generate more margin in your life.

Music stimulates both hemispheres of the brain simultaneously (actually no other activity seems to do this better than music); however there are some benefits to being able to switch between left-brain and right-brain. Ronald A. Berk of Johns Hopkins University suggests music is effective in isolating the side of the brain you wish to develop. To improve the function of your left-hemisphere, Berk recommends that you listen to unfamiliar, fast, up-tempo music in major keys. As we have read many times over, to relax the mind it is best to feed it with your preferences. However when we are working to stimulate and challenge the mind (stimulate your logic) using new music, that the brain needs to digest, can be effective. To work the right side of the brain (like when you are reading, studying, reflecting or engaging in creative pursuits) Berk suggests you want the exact opposite, slow music in minor keys. Slow, minor-key produce Alpha waves; these relax the brain, which can be useful and help your new experiences or learning pass into long-term memory.[18]

The music industry has proof that you should listen to music while you work. In a survey commissioned by the UK licensing organizations PPL and PRS for Music, 77 percent of surveyed businesses say playing music in the workplace increases staff morale and improves the atmosphere. The results seemed to be greater productivity. However a summary of recent research from Taiwan shows while some background music can increase worker satisfaction and productivity, music with lyrics could have significant negative effects on concentration and attention. The study concluded that music without lyrics is preferable, as lyrics are likely to reduce worker attention and performance.[19]

A 2010 study published in the Journal of Occupational and Environmental Medicine found employees with moderate sleep problems cost their companies about $2,500 in lost productivity a year. This study has also shown that listening to soft, slow (about 60 beats per minute) music like jazz or classical can improve the quality and duration of sleep, as well as improve functioning the next day. Research in business seems to also support such a claim. For example, a trial where 75 out of 256 workers at a large retail company were issued with personal stereos to wear at work for four weeks showed a 10 percent increase in productivity for the headphone wearers. Other similar research conducted by researchers at the University of Illinois found a 6.3 percent increase when compared with the no music control group.[20]

Research is quite clear on this point: if music improves your mood then your productivity will also be improved. So if we accept that music does increase productivity, does it matter what types of music we listen to? Does all music have the same effect or are certain types better in certain circumstances? The answer: our body's reaction to the music we choose to listen to, be it toes tapping, improved focus or inspired creativity are the key indicators that the music is working.

Exercise: Make Music Work at Work

There is no easy solution to developing a productive playlist for two or more people. Like all good work procedures and strategies, it takes time and it starts with being proactive instead of reactive. Take the time to identify the diverse needs and cultures of the group you belong to. Here are four suggested rules that are helpful when selecting music for your group:

1. discuss the benefits of playing music with your specific group

2. organize a forum where everyone can discuss their list of preferences

3. identify a compilation of benign music

4. set guidelines around when the music will be played

The benefits of playing music at work are numerous but they are different for everyone. For the employer, it may be boosting efficiency, expediting projects, and working with greater enthusiasm. For the staff member, it may be sparking creativity or help for working through a barrier in a project. For others it may be feeling better connected to others. Keep in mind that not everyone feels more productive, creative, or inspired when listening to music. Instead, they may feel distracted, stalled, or annoyed. This is the primary reason why it is important to start with honest discussion that includes all team members.

Preferences are important in assessing major triggers. I learned from one staff member that her boyfriend swears by heavy metal when he's racing to meet a deadline. On the other hand, she needs to crank out the show tunes when she wants to lose herself in her work. Clearly, everyone has different preferences when listening to music at work. When you meet with your group of two or more, start by making a list of all the music that everyone feels would suit the environment of their shared space. This request moves music from the realm of personal preferences to that of the larger group experience. For the employer or manager, this exercise can reveal the staff's perception of company culture and working environment.

Remember to not only address artists but also genres that suit the majority of the people. This includes music styles such as jazz, rock, blues, and classical. You can then get more specific. Once you have a board full of music that includes everyone's point of view you are ready to move on to the next stage.

In my experience there are certain music selections that tend to fall in the range of "benign music," ones that invokes the response of, "Oh that's an okay song" rather than "Oh I can't stand that group." Playing through the entire album of Supertramp may not be for everyone (it certainly isn't for me, obviously!)

Review your long list of music, including artists and genres, and work as a team to identify the oh-that's-okay "benign music." Setting guidelines of when music is played can be the most important part of the entire process, especially for those who work best in silence. There are many options of when but the most important part is that everyone agrees to the use of music in your environment.

Here are some suggestions for when:

- for the duration of everyone's set lunch time i.e. 11:30 a.m. to 1:30 p.m. to add a social component to the lunch

- the last hour of each day to pick up the mood and to signal the end of a successful day, thus promoting a boost in enthusiasm and a feeling of relaxation prior to going home.

- To celebrate various occasions. For example, for one hour on the day of someone's birthday, allow the birthday person or the co-workers to choose the playlist representing the birthday person.

- Play music throughout the day at a low volume with an increase in volume during brain-storming sessions

- Use silence throughout the day and allow individuals to use their own headsets for the music that makes them feel most vibrant at work

- during a presentation at a time when you want to capture a specific mood or give a big launch to a new product or idea

Keep in mind that if your workplace chooses to go the route of using your own playlists throughout the office instead of just listening to the radio, you will need to purchase a broadcast license agreement for background music. The small cost of this service gives our favourite composers and songwriters the royalties they are entitled to receive.

When new people start working with your company your playlist may need to be tweaked, but perhaps not as much as you think. People you hire will most likely be of a similar demographic and background of your other staff. What may need to happen is a bi-annual shake up—adding new selections to charge up the list. This could be something the entire team looks forward to working on together as a team-building exercise.

Take time to review the benefits, identify your team's preferences, find the music that suits your environment, and administer at the best times throughout the day. Fortunately for me, I do all my administrative work from a private office so I don't have to worry about disturbing cubicle mates when I want to sing along to the cast of Glee. The most important part about music with others is to respect one another's choices and music needs. Like my reaction to James in the car, sometimes our auditory triggers are fast and furious. Be kind to others so they don't feel they need to "sound off."

TUNE IN

Throughout the book, I have given you ways to use music more pro-actively in your life. In this last section I have given you strategies and exercises to use at home, work and leisure. To TUNE IN means to dig deeper, to go inside, to take a moment and reflect, to internalize something that makes you feel something more. Although this book was ultimately written to educate and inform you about the powerful benefits of using music in today's stress induced society, it is also meant to help you TUNE IN deeper to all things: your family, your friends, your work, your leisure. For it is my wish that you find ways to use music to enhance your life—in every possible way.

Endnote

Granny outlived Grandad by many years. I completed my education, moved away, and did not see her as often as I would have liked. However, her influence and direction were always with me.

Grandad may have taught me that grumpy people have favourite songs, but it was Granny with her request for me to play, her gentle hand on my shoulder, and her act of pulling up a chair for others that taught me how to build meaningful experiences through music, not just for myself, but for others to enjoy too.

Playing music at Grandad's bedside was the first time I experienced a deeper purpose for music. It wasn't the first time I had listened to music or been affected by music, but it was the first time I saw that music was capable of being more than just entertainment or a learning opportunity. If Granny had not asked, I never would have considered singing for Grandad. I did not anticipate his response, and I certainly had no idea that the trajectory of my life would change from that point on, growing into the symphony of stories I have written throughout this book.

It was Granny who encouraged me to become a Music Therapist. It was Granny who had me over for a cheesecake and a hug when I needed it. It was Granny who wrote my recommendation letter for University and who invited me many years later to come and bring my guitar to her Seniors Lodge to entertain her and her friends.

She always said, "It's so nice you took time to learn those old songs." What she didn't realize was how much she was responsible for introducing me to a period of music that I would have been denied if it wasn't for her. Because of Granny, I fell in love with the music of the twenties, thirties, and forties. It was her toe tapping to "Darktown Strutters Ball," and "Tennessee Waltz" that cemented my desire to keep going.

Those are just some of the thoughts that flashed through my mind when I received the call that Granny had suffered a serious stroke and that "it didn't look good." My sister and I immediately went to see her.

The hospital room was a place I was now quite familiar with after all the other seniors I have had an opportunity to visit and help transition from this life into the next. However, this room looked different. Someone I knew—someone I loved—was lying in the bed in front of me.

Granny looked fragile and thin. Her face drooped on the right side. I remember looking down on her small body and beautiful face, drained pale, saying as cheerfully as I could, "Hey, what's a good looking broad like you doing in a joint like this?"

Her face crinkled slightly and I heard a just audible "ha ha ha." I knew then that all would not be well. Granny was right there with us, but we were going to have to say goodbye.

My sister and I sat on either side of her and told her how much we loved her, what a great woman she was, and how much she had helped us through difficult times in our lives. She gave us an entire lifetime of support from our parents' divorce and struggles during our school years, to helping us with our marriages and balancing work and home life. We assured her it was something we would never be able to do as well as her. We told her how she taught us so many important things and especially what good caregiving really is. We said, "You are one tough act to follow."

It was somewhere during these endearments that my sister looked at me with tears in her eyes and said the unimaginable, "Jennifer, I think you should sing." It was unimaginable because I realized then that I had no voice. A song would make this all the more real. How was I going to say goodbye to Granny?

I froze. I was okay when I was talking but I knew I would not be able to sing and hold it together. I was certainly not going to cry in front of Granny. I wanted to be as strong for her as she had always been for me.

I looked at the woman who changed my life, who gave me music in a new way, and who believed in me. If I sang now I was essentially saying goodbye, and I wasn't ready to do that.

I felt a huge lump in my throat when I realized my sister had already started without me. With tears down her cheeks, she was singing. My sister never sang. After one familiar line, Granny started singing with her in a quiet voice. Granny was granting us one more gift—her voice— this song—just thirty-six hours before she would pass away. I will forever hold this memory close to my heart:

"You are my sunshine, my only sunshine.
You make me happy, when skies are grey.
You'll never know dear, how much I love you.
Please don't take my sunshine away."

Although one of the most requested songs in my career, I can honestly say that because of my relationship with this song, I always sing it as an anthem, a tribute to a woman I loved dearly. It is a celebration of all those who teach us what is really important in our lives.

It took a few minutes but I found my voice. I started to sing with them—

Goodbye Granny.

I love you.

"When we TUNE IN we feel more relaxed about work, home, and life.
When we TUNE IN we feel healthier.
When we TUNE IN we are more connected to those around us.
The key is the intention and the love in which we use it."
- Jennifer Buchanan

Gratitudes

My heartfelt thanks goes to Dr. Patricia Ross of Hugo House Publishers who first uttered the words, "you need to write that down." With her enthusiastic support and inspirational approach she has helped me realize a dream I didn't even know I had. I will forever be grateful.

Appreciation to my sister Andrea Lifton from Creative Lift for seeing the value of this book and helping me take it to the next level. I must acknowledge my music therapy mentor, Fran Herman, and the foundational work she gave our profession and on which this entire book is based. You continue to teach me about what this work is really about—the people we serve.

To my best friends, colleagues and teachers who took time to review this book, discuss this book and love me through it all—Janet Fedor, Fiona McColl, Jacqueline Peters, Cindy Chambers and my dear neighbour Caireen Likely. And to my 'Master Team' (Russ Dantu, Marco Iafrate and Krista Hermanson) I am forever grateful for your monthly words of encouragement and brilliant direction.

To the delightful music therapy colleague's "the conference girls" in my life that laugh with me, cry with me, support me and even on occasion drink scotch with me—without you the music therapy profession would not be as good nor nearly as fun and rewarding. Special mentions to Dr. Laurel Young for all the years of rooming with me at said conference - you are a dear friend and Noreen Donnell, for our annual run/walk the morning after the best party of the year.

Special thanks to Shannon Robinson it is a joy to work with you each day. To the entire JB Music Therapy team, it is you who continue to stretch me every day by the level of dedication and skill you put into your work. And I would remiss not to give a shout out to Melanie Mcdonald and Erin Gross—for although you have graduated from the team you have been nothing short of completely supportive of me and this company—it's almost like you never really defected.

To my dearest friend Debbie Lake for always knowing when I need a check in and a movie/shopping/bellini intervention.

Thank you to all the individuals featured in this book, current and past clients, for without your inspiration and teachings of what is possible through music I would not have been able to write this book.

To my mom—there are no words except I love you.

To Merrick and Braedan you both continually show me the good in life. Sometimes I hear so many sad stories in a day but then I come home and get to see you. You are pure joy and I am delighted to see what stellar human beings you have become.

And James. Your solicited and unsolicited advice was exactly what I needed. You challenge me and hug me exactly when I need it most. I simply would not have been able to write this book without you by my side. I love you.

Disclaimer

Please note that all exercises in this book are geared towards you experiencing something positive. If at anytime you access a memory that is not positive and you begin to feel troubled please contact a professional who can help you through it. Recommended professionals include: family physicians, psychologists, secular or spiritual ministers, and Music Therapists.

The names of all the clients throughout this book have been altered and in some cases characteristics have been modified to ensure anonymity of the client. It is my intention to ensure that everyone in this book is respectfully reflected for the beautiful music beings they are.

About the Author

Presenting to health care agencies, professional groups, family care-givers and educators, Jennifer Buchanan is a recognized expert on the wellness benefits of music for children, adults, and seniors.

Jennifer is instrumental in the implementation of hundreds of music therapy programs through her well-established company - JB Music Therapy - and its talented team of professional Music Therapists. She is the President of the Canadian Association for Music Therapy (1998 - 2001 and 2013-2015), has contributed her expertise on many professional boards, and happily guest lectured for universities, agencies and conferences in Canada and abroad.

In addition to her first major work, TUNE IN, Jennifer has contributed to the text books Creating Connections in Nursing Care Through the Arts and the Autism Handbook 101.

Jennifer is a proud member of the Global Speaker's Federation and the Canadian Association of Professional Speakers. She lives in Canada with her husband, adult children, her dog Agatha, and, of course, her guitar.

For more information on Jennifer Buchanan, please visit
www.jenniferbuchanan.ca

I sing my heart out to the infinite sea
I sing my vision to the sky-high mountains
I sing my song to the free.
- Pete Townshend, "Song is Over"

References, Notes and Links

First Note

1. The "White Cliffs of Dover," was a popular World War II song made famous by Vera Lynn in 1942. Written by Walter Kent and Nat Burton in 1941, the song was written before America joined World War II to uplift the spirits of the Allies at a time when Nazi Germany had conquered much of Europe. The actual white cliffs form part of the British coastline that face the Strait of Dover and France.

About TUNE IN

1. There is also evidence to indicate that work stress causes 10% of all strokes.Suadicani P1, Andersen LL, Holtermann A, Mortensen OS, Gyntelberg F. Perceived psychological pressure at work, social class, and risk of stroke: a 30-year follow-up in Copenhagen male study. J Occup Environ Med. 2011 Dec;53(12):1388-95.
    http://www.livescience.com/36038-work-stress-stroke-risk.html)

2. and that 3 out of 4 doctor's visits are for stress-related ailments. Schnall, Peter L. Unhealthy Work: Causes, Consequences, Cures. Amityville, N.Y.: Baywood Pub., 2009.
    http://www.huffingtonpost.com/joe-robinson/stress-and-health_b_3313606.html

3. The researchers estimated that a potential savings of $2.25 billion per year could be saved if music therapy was used throughout the United States during such procedures.
    DeLoach Walworth D. Procedural-support music therapy in the healthcare setting: A cost-effectiveness analysis. J Ped Nursing. 2005;20(4):276-84.

4. The cost savings when using music therapy showed a reduction of $567 per procedure. Wood B. CT scans and radiation exposure. AAP Grand Rounds. 2008;19:28-9.

Chapter 1: The Power of Music

1. When we respond positively to the music we are listening to we are more
    likely to improve our performance on certain tasks, our imagination is
    peaked, and our emotional state is altered.
    "The Psychology of Musical Preferences." Psychology Today. Accessed
    March 30, 2015.
    https://www.psychologytoday.com/blog/mr-personality/201101/the-psy-
    chology-musical-preferences)

2. Brad suffered from severe Post Traumatic Stress Disorder (PTSD)
    Post-Traumatic stress disorder is a type of anxiety disorder. It can occur
    after you've seen or experienced a traumatic event that involved the threat
    of injury or death. Many veterans returning from a war often have PTSD.
    It is not known why traumatic events cause PTSD in some people but not
    others.
    http://www.ncbi.nlm.nih.gov/pubmedhealth/PMH0001923/

3. ...and chronic depression (also known as Dysthymia)
    The main symptom of dysthymia is a low, dark, or sad mood on most days
    for at least two years. In children and adolescents, the mood can be irri-
    table instead of depressed and may last for at least one year. People with
    dysthymia will often take a negative or discouraging view of themselves,
    their future, other people, and life events. Problems often seem more diffi-
    cult to solve.
    http://www.ncbi.nlm.nih.gov/pubmedhealth/PMH0001916/

4. Terrance Hays and Victor Minichiello, have written extensively about the
    contribution of music to self-identity and quality of life.
    Hays T., Minichiello V. (2005). The meaning of music in the lives of older
    people: a qualitative study. Psychol. Music 33, 437–451

5. Today, I know I was affected by a mild case of postpartum depression
    Women commonly have mood changes during pregnancy, especially
    after delivery. These mood changes may be caused by changes in hor-
    mone levels. Feelings of anxiety, irritation, tearfulness, and restlessness
    are common in the week or two after pregnancy. These feelings are often
    called the postpartum or "baby blues." These symptoms almost always go

away without the need for treatment.

http://www.ncbi.nlm.nih.gov/pubmedhealth/PMH0004481/

6. I do question whether there is something else happening. It would seem to me that music's capacity to reflect and evoke emotions and memories, some deeply hidden, may have something to do with the choice to live without any music.

    Ernest Mas-Herrero, Robert J. Zatorre, Antoni Rodriguez-Fornells, Josep Marco-Pallarés. Dissociation between Musical and Monetary Reward Responses in Specific Musical Anhedonia. Current Biology, 06 March 2014

7. Donna's dad had Alzheimer's Disease

    Alzheimer's disease is an irreversible, progressive brain disease that slowly destroys memory-thinking skills and eventually limits even the ability to carry out the simplest tasks. In most people with Alzheimer's, symptoms first appear after age sixty. Estimates vary but experts suggest that as many as 5.1 million Americans may have Alzheimer's disease.

    http://www.alz.org/alzheimers_disease_what_is_alzheimers._asp

8. Each month, Donna took her dad to a senior's centre for a "drum circle." In the words of Arthur Hull: "The Community Drum Circle is a fun entry-level learning experience that is accessible to anyone who wants to participate. Drum Circle participants express themselves collectively by using a chorus of tuned drums, percussion, and vocals to create a song together while having a great time.

9. A person's ability to engage in music, such as drumming and singing, remains intact late into the disease process because these activities do not require cognitive functioning for feelings of achievement.

    "Alzheimer's Foundation of America." Alzheimer's Foundation of America. Accessed March 31, 2015.

    http://www.alzfdn.org/EducationandCare/musictherapy.html

10. Her wide set eyes and low muscle tone indicated that she had some extra DNA on her 21st chromosome, better known as Down Syndrome.

    Down syndrome occurs when there is an extra copy of chromosome 21. This form of Down syndrome is called Trisomy 21. The extra chromosome causes problems with the way the body and brain develop. Down syn-

drome is the most common single cause of human birth defects.
http://www.ncbi.nlm.nih.gov/pubmedhealth/PMH0001992/

11. Missing some DNA on his 7th chromosome, Warren had Williams Syndrome
Williams Syndrome (WS) is a rare genetic disorder characterized by mild
to moderate cognitive deficit or learning difficulties, a distinctive facial
appearance, and a unique personality that combines over-friendliness and
high levels of empathy with anxiety. The most significant medical problem
associated with WS is cardiovascular disease caused by narrowed arteries. A random genetic mutation (deletion of a small piece of chromosome
7), rather than inheritance, most often causes the disorder.
http://www.ninds.nih.gov/disorders/williams/williams.htm

12. Some studies suggest health care dollars would be saved if music was
used in the care of individuals.
Cohen, Gene. "New theories and research findings on the positive influence of music and art on health with aging." Arts and Health (March 2009):
48 – 62.
http://www.tandfonline.com/doi/abs/10.1080/17533010802528033

A multi-state, two year study in the U.S., published in the journal Arts and
Health in February 2009, monitored medication usage of two groups—one
group that resided in long term care and one group that resided in long
term care and participated in a regular group music program three times
per week. The participants in the music program three times per week
reported a higher overall rating of physical health, fewer doctor's visits,
less medication used, and fewer instances of falls compared to the control
group. The author of the study suggests that if all persons who fall under
what is classified as Medicare D (national health coverage for those aged
sixty-five and older in the U.S.) participated in the music program with similar results as in the stud— then the savings would equal 6.3 billion dollars.

13. Listening to music was also found to be more effective than prescription
drugs in reducing anxiety prior to surgery, a drug with little side effects.
Chanda, Mona Lisa, and Daniel J. Levitin. "The Neurochemistry of Music."
Trends in Cognitive Sciences: 179-93.
https://www.mcgill.ca/newsroom/channels/news/major-health-bene-

fits-music-uncovered-225589

14. Having the right resources available and the knowledge that this brief exercise can boost productivity by reducing stress may be helpful.
"The Power of Music To Reduce Stress." Psych Central.com. Accessed March 31, 2015.
http://psychcentral.com/lib/the-power-of-music-to-reduce-stress/000930

Chapter 2: The Value of Music

1. "I've Got the Music in Me" is a song by The Kiki Dee Band, released in 1974. It was written in 1973 by Bias Boshell, Kiki Dee Band's keyboardist. The song entered the UK Singles Chart on September 7, 1974, reached number nineteen and stayed on the charts for eight weeks.

2. Music helps us to feel connected to our feelings, our environment, or the people around us—to feel connected to a bigger experience, a memory, or a person we love.
Baumgartner, Hans (1992), "Remembrance of Things Past; Music, Autobiographical Memory, and Emotion." Advances in Consumer Research. Eds. John F. Sherry, Jr. and Brian Sternthal. Association for Consumer Research. 19 (1992): 613 – 620.
http://www.acrwebsite.org/volumes/display.asp?id=7363

3. Humans make decisions based on emotion and then construct the logic behind these decisions. A few years ago, neuroscientist Antonio Damasio made a groundbreaking discovery.
Damasio, Antonio R. Descartes' Error: Emotion, Reason, and the Human Brain. New York: Putnam, 1994.

4. Sixties rock superstar Jimi Hendrix said: "You can hypnotize people with music, and when you get them at their weakest point, you can preach into their subconscious whatever you want to say."
Jimi Hendrix was an American guitarist and singer-songwriter. He is widely considered to be the greatest electric guitarist in music history.

5. Music can focus us on a task by relaxing our mind and allowing our subconscious to manage some of the work
Cockerton, T., Moore, S., & Norman, D. (1997). "Cognitive test performance

and background music." Perceptual and Motor Skills 85 (1997): 1435 – 1438.

Rauscher, F. H., Shaw, G. L., & Ky, K. N. (1993). "Music and spatial task performance." Nature 365 (1993): 611.

6. Hallman, S., Price, J. & Katsarou, G. (2002). T"he effects of background music on primary school pupil' task performance." Educational Studies 28 (2002): 111 – 122.

   Research seems to support such a claim. For example, a trial where 75 out of 256 workers at a large retail company were issued with personal stereos to wear at work for four weeks showed a 10 percent increase in productivity for the headphone wearers. Other similar research conducted by researchers at the University of Illinois found a 6.3 percent increase when compared with the no music control group.

   http://www.articlesbase.com/self-help-articles/can-listening-to-music-help-us-work-better-68598.html

7. However, there is some research that indicates that new information is best done with the music off.

   "Can Preference for Background Music Mediate the Irrelevant Sound Effect?" Nick Perham, et. al.; Applied Cognitive Psychology; Published Online: July 20, 2010

   http://ca.wiley.com/WileyCDA/PressRelease/pressReleaseId-79057.html

8. When you listen to music that moves you your brain releases dopamine that makes you feel extra good and when we feel good it becomes easier to feel positive connections to others around us. "Why Music Makes You Happy : DNews." DNews. Accessed March 31, 2015.

   http://news.discovery.com/human/psychology/music-dopamine-happiness-brain-110110.htm

9. With dementia, repetition is even more important if Heath hopes to feel connected with Sarah and celebrate what they have had.

   Hellen C., Padilla R. "Working with Elders Who Have Dementia and Alzheimer's Disease." New York : Psychology Press. 2011.

   http://ot.creighton.edu/community/OT_FOR_ELDERS/3rd_Edition_Chapters/Proofs/Padilla_Chapter_20_main.pdf

10. In the book The Power of Music, Elena Mannes highlights how music
    affects different groups of people.
    Mannes, Elena. The Power of Music: Pioneering Discoveries in the New
    Science of Song. New York: Walker &, 2011.
    http://www.npr.org/2011/06/01/136859090/the-power-of-music-to-affect-
    the-brain

11. In 1959 a doctor named Teirich undertook one of the earliest studies into
    the therapeutic effects of music and vibration.
    Teirich, H.R. (1959). On therapeutics through music and vibrations. In H.
    Scherchen (Ed.) Gravesaner Blatter , (pp.1-14). Mainz: Ars Viva Verlag.

12. If music was able to relax such a diverse group of individuals, suffering
    with day-to-day anxieties and stress, serious enough that they were need-
    ing hospital support, just imagine how one of your stressful day could be
    turned around by just a simple musical exercise.

13. Allen K. et al. Normalization of hypertensive responses during ambulatory
    surgical stress by perioperative music. Psychosomatic Medicine, 63 (May/
    June 2001) 487 – 492. Print.

14. Waldon E. G. The effects of group music therapy on mood states and
    cohesiveness in adult oncology patients. Journal of Music Therapy 38 (Fall
    2001) 212 – 238. Print. Collingwood, J. "The Power of Music To Reduce
    Stress." Psych Central. 2007. Web. June 7, 2012.
    http://psychcentral.com/ lib/2007/the-power-of-music-to-reduce-stress.

15. There have been tremendous results in speech rehabilitation using a tech-
    nique known as melodic intonation therapy.
    Norton, Andrea et al. "Melodic Intonation Therapy: Shared Insights on How
    It Is Done and Why It Might Help." Annals of the New York Academy of
    Sciences1169 (2009): 431–436. PMC. Web. 31 Mar. 2015.
    http://www.ncbi.nlm.nih.gov/pmc/articles/PMC2780359/

16. In the spring that year, I received a call that Don Felder, formerly of the
    Eagles www.donfelder.com

17. Some people believe that music was important to human evolution, from
    how infants develop language to how we pass down information to new
    generations.

"This Is Your Brain On Music." Medical Daily. Accessed March 31, 2015. http://www.medicaldaily.com/your-brain-music-how-our-brains-process-melodies-pull-our-heartstrings-271007

18. In her book, she likens silence to oil, something that needs to be sourced and mined in order to capture its power of transformation—one of life's greatest commodities.
Lees, Helen E. Silence in Schools. Stoke on Trent: Trentham Books/IOE Press, 2012.
http://www.amazon.com/Silence-Schools-Helen-Lees/dp/1858564751

19. The research is clear that three deep breathes can reduce your fight or flight response.
"Dr. Herbert Benson's Relaxation Response." Psychology Today. Accessed March 31, 2015.
https://www.psychologytoday.com/blog/heart-and-soul-healing/201303/dr-herbert-benson-s-relaxation-response

Chapter 3: Triggers and Anchors

1. The ability to perceive emotion in music develops early in childhood, and changes throughout development.
Dowling, W. J. (2002). "The development of music perception and cognition". Foundations of Cognitive Psychology: Core Reading: 481–502.

2. Just as different people perceive events differently, based upon their past experiences, emotions elicited by listening to different types of music are affected due to personal, previous experiences.Ladinig, Olivia; Schellenberg, E. Glenn (1 January 2012). "Liking unfamiliar music: Effects of felt emotion and individual differences.".Psychology of Aesthetics, Creativity, and the Arts 6 (2): 146–154.

3. While some studies indicate that music training is correlated with high music intelligence as well as higher IQ....
Schellenberg, E. Glenn; Mankarious, Monika (1 January 2012). "Music training and emotion comprehension in childhood.". Emotion 12 (5): 887–891.

4. ...other studies refute the claim.

Kratus, J. (1 January 1993). "A Developmental Study of Children's Interpretation of Emotion in Music". Psychology of Music 21 (1): 3–19.

5. However what is worth noting is that exposure to music earlier in life seems to affect behavioral choices, schoolwork, and social interactions later in life.
"Impact of Music, Music Lyrics, and Music Videos on Children and Youth". PEDIATRICS 124 (5): 1488–1494. 19 October 2009.

6. As we have identified, stress contributes to many human diseases. Carnegie Mellon University. "Stress Contributes To Range Of Chronic Diseases, Review Shows." ScienceDaily Oct 9, 2007. Web. 3 Jun. 2012. http://www.sciencedaily.com/releases/2007/10/071009164122.

7. I tried concentrating on browsing my smart phone and contemplated updating my Facebook status
@jbmusictherapy

8. A playlist is simply a list of songs. They can be played sequentially or in a shuffled order.
Dan Goleman, in his bestseller Emotional Intelligence, calls this action "an amygdala highjacking."
Goleman, Daniel. Emotional Intelligence. New York: Bantam Books, 1995. http://blogs.psychcentral.com/parenting-tips/2013/07/uncovering-emotional-triggers-or-where-did-my-brain-just-go/

9. The Young Offenders Centre was at the far edge of town.
Also known as a juvenile detention centre. A secured residential facility for young people awaiting court hearings or fulfilling their sentencing.

10. In one study researchers presented excerpts of fast tempo, major mode music and slow tempo, and minor mode music to participants. These musical structures were chosen because they have been proven to convey happiness and sadness respectively.

11. Hunter, P. G.; Schellenburg, E. G.; Schimmack, U. (2010). "Feelings and perceptions of happiness and sadness induced by music: Similarities, differences, and mixed emotions". Psychology of Aesthetics, Creativity, and the Arts 4: 47–56.

12. A Neuroscientist was a patient at his own clinic being prepped for spinal surgery.
Carr, Coeli. "Using music to ease patient stress during surgery." Time.com. 13 Oct. 2009. Web. June 1, 2012.
http://www.time.com/time/health/article/0,8599,1929994,00. html

13. However, there is indication that surgeons are not asking others in the operating room for their preferences: one survey of anesthetists found that about a quarter felt that music "reduced their vigilance and impaired their communication with other staff," and about half felt that music was distracting when they were dealing with a problem with the anesthesia.
"Does Listening to Music While Working Make You Less Productive?" Ideas Does Listening to Music While Working Make You Less Productive Comments. Accessed March 31, 2015.
http://ideas.time.com/2012/09/12/does-listening-to-music-while-working-make-you-less-productive/

14. In the context of this book, your music library is all the music you have encountered throughout your lifetime.

Chapter 4: Fnd Your Music

1. However, under the right circumstances all music is retrievable meaning that it's something that we can remember when the conditions are right.
Williamon A. & Egner T. "Memory structures for encoding and retrieving a piece of music: an ERP investigation." Cognitive Brain Research, 22: 36 – 44.
http://lib.bioinfo.pl/paper:15561499

2. I have read magazines that suggest we don't add much new music after the age of thirty.
Hyden S. & Murray N. "Why do pop-culture fans stop caring about new music as they get older?" A.V. Club. May 10, 2011. Web. Jan 15, 2012.
http://www.avclub.com/articles/why-do-popculture-fans-stop-caring-about-new-music,55805/

3. If you have young children in your life, I want to pause for a moment and review a few important details. From as early as in our mother's womb

there is evidence that babies are aware of and respond to music and different sounds.

Tan S., Pfordresher P., and Harre R. "Psychology of Music: From Sound of Significance." New York: Psychology Press, 2010

http://www.psypress.com/common/sample-chapters/9781841698687.pdf

4. There is great evidence around the connection of stimuli being received in early childhood and brain growth.

    Society For Neuroscience. "New Studies Show Factors Respon- sible For Enhanced Response To Music." ScienceDaily, 13 Nov. 2003. Web. 6 Jun. 2012.

    http://www.sciencedaily.com/releases/2003/11/031113065626.htm

5. There is enough evidence to say that our musical preferences start forming before the age of two.

    Fagen, J., Prigot, J., Carroll, M., Pioli, L., Stein, A., & Franco, A. (1997). Auditory context and memory retrieval in young infants. Child Development 68 (1997): 1057 – 1066.

    Rauscher, F. H., Shaw, G. L., Levine, L. J., Wright, E. L., Dennis, W. R., & Newcomb, R. L. Music training causes long-term enhancement of pre-school children's spatial-temporal reasoning. Neurological Research 19 (1997): 2 – 8.

    Viadero, D. "Music on the Mind". Education Week, April 8, 1998

    Wallace, W. T. (1994). "Memory for music: Effect of melody on recall of text." Journal of Experimental Psychology: Learning, Memory & Cognition 20 (1994) 1471 – 1485.

6. The brain undergoes rapid neural development during the first years of life and new neural networks are formed more rapidly than at any other time.

    Casey B.J., Tottenham N., Liston C., Durston S. "Imaging the developing brain: what have we learned about cognitive development?" Trends in Cognitive Sciences 9.3 (March 2005): 104 – 110.

    http://www.sciencedirect.com/science/article/pii/S1364661305000306

7. The brain goes through many processes helping us interpret the music that we hear. Our ears become attuned to certain styles and textures which are specifically intriguing to us.

    Levitin, Daniel J. This is Your Brain on Music: The Science of a Human

Obsession. New York: Dutton/Penguin, 2006.
http://www.amazon.ca/This-Your-Brain-Music-Obsession/
dp/0452288525.

8. There is a long held theory that the subconscious mind can recognize patterns within complex data and that we are hardwired to find simple patterns pleasurable.
BioMed Central. "Creating simplicity: How music fools the ear." Science-Daily, 20. Jan. 2011 Web. 6 June 2012.
http://www.biomedcentral.com/1756-0500/4/9/abstract

9. Studies show music can actually lower your heart rate and reduce stress for some people.
Davis, W.B., & Thaut, M.H. "The influence of preferred relaxing music on measures of state anxiety, relaxation, and physiological responses." Journal of Music Therapy 26 (1989): 168 – 187.
Hyde IM, Scalapino W. The influence of music upon electro-cardiograms and blood pressure. Am J Physiol. 46 (1918): 35 – 38.
Joseph CN, Porta C, Casucci G, Casiraghi N, Maffeis M, Rossi M, Bernardi L. Slow "Breathing improves arterial baroreflex sensitivity and decreases blood pressure in essential hypertension." Hypertension. 46 (2005) 714 – 718.

10. Bernardi P, Porta C, Sleight P. Cardiovascular, cerebrovascular and respiratory changes induced by different types of music in musicians and non-musicians: the importance of silence. Heart. 92 (2006) 445 – 452.

Chapter 5: Maximize Your Music

1. People have long known that music can trigger powerful recollections, but now brain-scan studies show us what is really happening and why when we use the right music we can actually help keep our memories in good working order. The part of the brain known as the medial pre-frontal cortex sits just behind the forehead. Petr Janata, a cognitive neuroscientist at University of California describes what is happening.
Hsu, By. "Music-Memory Connection Found in Brain." LiveScience. February 24, 2009. Accessed March 31, 2015.

http://www.livescience.com/5327-music-memory-connection-brain.html

2. Dr. Daniel Levitin has proven that listening to music releases certain chemicals in the brain.
    Chanda, Mona Lisa, and Daniel J. Levitin. "The Neurochemistry of Music." Trends in Cognitive Sciences: 179-93.
    http://daniellevitin.com/levitinlab/articles/2013-TICS_1180.pdf

3. People have different emotional reactions to the same music. A random sample of 540 Spanish consumers (aged fifteen to sixty-five), were played a series of radio advertisements for a fictitious mineral water.
    Vanessa Apaolaza-Ibáñez, Mark Zander, Patrick Hartmann. "Memory, emotions and rock 'n' roll: The influence of music in advertising, on brand and endorser perception." African Journal of Business Management 4.17 (2010): 3805 – 3816.
    http://www.sciencedaily.com/releases/2011/06/110622045135.htm

4. The other half of the participants listened to twelve random excerpts five times, and started their ratings on the third repetition. Participants who listened to the excerpts five times rated their emotions with higher intensity than the participants who listened to them only once.
    Ali, S. O.; Peynircioglu, Z. F. (2010). "Intensity of emotions conveyed and elicited by familiar and unfamiliar music". Music Perception: An Interdisciplinary Journal 27: 177–182.

5. Working with two sample groups of 240 volunteers over 60 years old, where one group took part in weekly singing sessions over three months and the other didn't, the research revealed an increase in the mental health component score on a validated health measure amongst the group of singers. It also revealed significantly reduced anxiety and depression scores.
    "Study into Benefits of Singing Proves Positive Impact on Health." Study into Benefits of Singing Proves Positive Impact on Health. Accessed March 31, 2015.
    http://medicalxpress.com/news/2012-08-benefits-positive-impact-health.html#jCp

6. Group drumming alters neuroendocrine and immunologic measurements

in the participants – this means a boost to your immune system. "Beating Stress -- on the Drums." WebMD. Accessed March 31, 2015. http://www.webmd.com/balance/stress-management/news/20010209/beating-stress----on-drums

7. According to a study published by the American Psychological Association, playing an instrument as a child keeps the mind sharper as we age. "The Relation Between Instrumental Musical Activity and Cognitive Aging," Brenda Hanna-Pladdy, PhD, and Alicia MacKay, PhD, University of Kansas Medical Center; Neuropsychology, Vol. 25, No. 3

8. Group lessons can take your experience to a whole new level. to go on your daily run or attend your weekly spin class, you should change things up, says Jordan Metzl, a sports medicine physician at the Hospital for Special Surgery in New York. "Trying something new that shakes up your routine can really give you a fresh perspective and get you excited," Dr. Metzl says.
"Shake Things Up: Why You Should Try New Ways to Exercise." WSJ. Accessed March 31, 2015.
http://www.wsj.com/articles/shake-things-up-why-you-should-try-new-ways-to-exercise-1425924098

9. Costas Karageorghis of Brunel University in London, one of the world's leading experts on the psychology of exercise music, wrote that one could think of music as a legal performance-enhancing drug. In truth, it looks like music can boost your athletic performance by 15%. There's more to it than distraction, music makes people less aware of their exertion. The music seems to propel them forward helping them get maximum benefit. Karageorghis, Costas I. ": Sport and Music for the Masses." Sport in Society: 433-47.
http://bura.brunel.ac.uk/handle/2438/6312

10. The rhythm of your workout music stimulates the motor area of the brain aiding in your movements and keeping them steady. This leads to a sense of greater efficiency since keeping a steady pace is easier on our bodies than fluctuating through the workout.
"Let's Get Physical: The Psychology of Effective Workout Music." Scientific American Global RSS. Accessed March 31, 2015.

http://www.scientificamerican.com/article/psychology-workout-music/

11. In an analysis of U.S. Department of Education data on more than 25,000 secondary school students (NELS:88, National Education Longitudinal Survey), researchers found that students who report consistent high levels of involvement in instrumental music over the middle and high school years show "significantly higher levels of mathematics proficiency by grade 12." This observation holds regardless of students' socio-economic status, and differences in those who are involved with instrumental music vs. those who are not is more significant over time.
Catterall, James S., Richard Chapleau, and John Iwanaga. "Involvement in the Arts and Human Development: General Involvement and Intensive Involvement in Music and Theater Arts." Los Angeles, CA: The Imagination Project at UCLA Graduate School of Education and Information Studies, 1999.

12. Music can: Relax the mind and lower stress levels.
Collingwood, Jayne. "The Power of Music To Reduce Stress." Psych Central.com. Accessed April 1, 2015.
http://psychcentral.com/lib/the-power-of-music-to-reduce-stress/000930

13. Music can: Stimulate creativity by increasing blood and oxygen flow to the brain – going from sleepy brain to teachable brain.
University of Maryland Medical Center. "Joyful Music May Promote Heart Health." ScienceDaily.
www.sciencedaily.com/releases/2008/11/081111182904.htm (accessed April 1, 2015).

14. Music can: Create a clear passage to long-term memory.
Jäncke, Lutz. "Music, Memory and Emotion." Journal of Biology, no. 7 (2008): 21.
http://jbiol.com/content/7/6/21

15. Music can: Change an individuals's emotional state
Changizi, Mark. "Why Does Music Make Us Feel?" Scientific American Global RSS. September 15, 2009. Accessed April 1, 2015.
http://www.scientificamerican.com/article/why-does-music-make-us-fe/

16. Nearly half of all workers suffer from moderate to severe stress while on

the job, according to a recent survey. And 66 percent of employees report that they have difficulty focusing on tasks at work because of stress. Stress has been called the "health epidemic of the 21st century" by the World Health Organization and it costs American businesses up to $300 billion a year.
https://www.mequilibrium.com/wp-content/uploads/2013/03/3-1-13-FI-NAL.pdf

17. A survey of 2,500 employees by ComPsych, a provider of employee assistance programs (EAPs), highlights the problem. In addition to the challenges related to focus at work, employees also said that stress was responsible for errors and/or missed deadlines (21 percent), trouble getting along with co-workers/superiors (15.5 percent), missed days (14.9 percent) and lateness (14.4 percent).
"Results By Industry." March 29, 2012. Accessed April 1, 2015.
http://www.compsych.com/press-room/media-cover-age-2012/575-march-29-2012

18. Slow, minor-key produce Alpha waves – these relax the brain, which can be useful and help your new.
Millbower, L. (2000). Training with a beat: The teaching power of music. Sterling, VA: Stylus

19. However a summary of recent research from Taiwan shows while some background music can increase worker satisfaction and productivity, music with lyrics could have significant negative effects on concentration and attention. The study concluded that music without lyrics is preferable, as lyrics are likely to reduce worker attention and performance.
Shih, YN. "Background Music: Effects on Attention Performance." WORK 42, no. 4 (2012): 573-8.
http://www.ncbi.nlm.nih.gov/pubmed/22523045

20. For example, a trial where 75 out of 256 workers at a large retail company were issued with personal stereos to wear at work for four weeks showed a 10% increase in productivity for the headphone wearers. Other similar research conducted by researchers at the University of Illinois found a 6.3% increase when compared with the no music control group.
Rosekind, Mark R., Kevin B. Gregory, Melissa M. Mallis, Summer L.

Brandt, Brian Seal, and Debra Lerner. "The Cost Of Poor Sleep: Workplace Productivity Loss And Associated Costs." Journal of Occupational and Environmental Medicine, 2010, 91-98. http://journals.lww.com/joem/Abstract/2010/01000 The_Cost_of_Poor_Sleep__Workplace_Productivity13.aspx

Made in the USA
Monee, IL
19 September 2020